A Spy's Wife

The Moscow Memoirs of a Canadian
Who Witnessed the End
of the Cold War

A Spy's Wife

The Moscow Memoirs of a Canadian Who Witnessed the End of the Cold War

Janice Cowan

James Lorimer & Company Ltd., Publishers
Toronto

Copyright © 2006 by Janice Cowan

All rights reserved. No part of this book may be reproduced or transmitted in any form or by any means, electronic or mechanical, including photocopying, or by any information storage or retrieval system, without permission in writing from the publisher.

James Lorimer & Company Ltd. acknowledges the support of the Ontario Arts Council. We acknowledge the support of the Government of Canada through the Book Publishing Industry Development Program (BPIDP) for our publishing activities. We acknowledge the support of the Canada Council for the Arts for our publishing program. We acknowledge the support of the Government of Ontario through the Ontario Media Development Corporation's Ontario Book Initiative.

Cover design: Meghan Collins

The Canada Council | Le Conseil des Arts
for the Arts | du Canada

ONTARIO ARTS COUNCIL
CONSEIL DES ARTS DE L'ONTARIO

Library and Archives Canada Cataloguing in Publication

Cowan, Janice
A spy's wife: the Moscow memoirs of a Canadian who witnessed the end of the cold war/ Janice Cowan.

ISBN10: 1-55028-931-4 (pbk.)
ISBN13: 978-1-55028-931-2 (pbk.)

I. Cowan, Janice. 2. Russia (Federation) --Politics and government --1991-. 3. Espionage, Canadian--Russia (Federation). 4. Spies' spouses--Russia (Federation)--Moscow--Biography. 5. Spies' spouses --Canada--Biography.
I. Title
DK593.c68 2006   947'.31086092   C2006-903633-0

James Lorimer & Company Ltd., Publishers
317 Adelaide Street West, Suite #1002
Toronto, Ontario
M5V 1P9
www.lorimer.ca

Printed and bound in Canada

Contents

1. Recruitment — 9
2. Spy School — 19
3. Working with Spooks — 26
4. In-Country — 45
5. Coup d'état — 55
6. "Friends" — 65
7. Cotton Country — 74
8. Stomaching the Facts — 79
9. Carpet Bagging — 87
10. Oil and Fire — 91

11.	Spies' Lies	98
12.	Shadowy Journalists	101
13.	Shooting Stars	110
14.	Zhiguli, Zhukov, and Japanese Socks	117
15.	Bugs and Bottles	128
16.	Kravchenko	137
17.	Chechnya	143
18.	Free Press and Ethics	154
19.	October Uprising	164
20.	Art of Diplomacy	180
21.	Brief Reunion	187
22.	Man from Gorky	193
23.	Spied Out	200

Although this is a factual account, some names, and other distinguishing information, have been altered to protect the privacy of individuals.

1

Recruitment

I was asked to become a spy while writing full time for *Frank* in Ottawa in late 1989. *Frank*, a nasty satirical magazine, attacked everything establishment—politicians, the media, the military, lawyers, and rich entrepreneurs. It would have been detested by the head of Canada's military intelligence, who interviewed me for the spy job.

Working for *Frank* was a different world from the military, though armed forces' morale at the time was low and provided us with many a "Deep Throat." But journalism is a good training ground if you are going to become a spy—prying into people's business, worming your way into their hearts, and sometimes attempting borderline blackmail to find the big story. That's the kind of journalism I learned in England in the sixties.

The CBC almost put an end to my spying career before it started. Shortly before my crucial interview, eager to learn who was writing the copy for *Frank*, the newest and most outspoken–some might say muckraking–magazine on the block, a CBC television reporter and cameraman surreptitiously filmed the scene inside the magazine's office from the third-floor hallway. It was the middle of the morning when they silently pushed open the mail slot in the office door and placed the lens of the camera up against the opening. The sneakiness was deliberate—after all, wasn't this how *Frank*'s no-name reporters collected their scoops?

David Bentley, the magazine's founder whom I had known since our cub reporting days in the UK, was in the front office; I was at a computer in a smaller room at the back. We were both too busy to hear or see the camera so I was startled when the TV crew, not wanting its cleverness to go unnoticed, burst through the door. David said later that if the Devil himself had walked in he probably wouldn't have paid much attention, so fraught were those early days of producing *Frank*. But hearing the confrontation with David and the mention of "CBC," I hid in a clothes closet.

I didn't want to raise any red flags by appearing on the evening news. Not with the invitation to become George Smiley for three years burning a hole in my pocket. Smiley, John Le Carré's wise and wary character, was the archetypical spy as far as I was concerned.

I don't know when my interest in the spy world first started, but I think it came to me naturally growing up in England at a time when the tabloids were rife with talk of Russian spies and defectors. The Cambridge spies, diplomats Guy Burgess and Donald Maclean, fled to Moscow in the fifties; Kim Philby, their foreign office colleague, followed them in the early sixties; George Blake, another ex-diplomat, was jailed for spying. Georgi Markov, a dissident Bulgarian, was killed at a bus stop on Waterloo Bridge when someone unkindly stabbed him in the leg with the ricin-poisoned tip of a British brolly. It seemed the Soviets did not like the broadcasts he was doing for the BBC. Then there was John Profumo, the unfortunate war minister who got caught up in a spy scandal when it was discovered he was visiting the same call girl as Eugene Ivanov, a naval attaché from the Soviet embassy in London. Prior to his downfall I'd met Profumo. Still only a teenager, I reported for the local paper on a visit the war minister made to Woking in Surrey.

During the height of the Cold War, perhaps to reassure themselves, Brits turned to humorous flights of fancy—romanticism rather than McCarthyism. Ian Fleming's *From Russia with Love* exploded onto movie screens, Michael Caine entertained as agent Harry Palmer in *The Ipcress File* and *Funeral in Berlin,* and the secret agents in *The Avengers* were the most popular characters on television. Former intelligence agent Le Carré achieved fame with *The Spy Who Came in from the Cold* and everyone thought he or she knew exactly what it was like to be an undercover operative.

It was while working for a local Surrey newspaper that I met my first Communists. They were officials from the National Union of Journalists who came down from London to lecture us on the brotherhood of the union. They addressed us as "Brother Smith" or "Sister Jones." We were young and laughed behind their backs. But they were serious—if they discovered a local press was not following union rules, they quickly called a strike and it was "everybody out." We were called "blacklegs" if we continued to work. It wasn't until Margaret Thatcher became prime minister in the late seventies that the union's power over publishers was curtailed. But by then I had already left for Canada.

I encountered my first Cold War Russians in the eighties. I was working as a reporter on a newspaper in New Brunswick. The Miramichi area of New Brunswick in that era was how I always imagined the Soviet Union. Clusters of wooden houses dotted alongside a big river. Primary industries, a foul-smelling paper mill, and a large military base. Working class. Heavy drinking. Illegal fishing. Domestic disputes. Miramichiers even used to take off for Moscow to see hockey games.

I saw the Russian fishing trawler tied up under Chatham's Centennial Bridge on my way home from work. Everyone knew the Soviets had two reasons for being on the Miramichi River—to catch Gaspereau fish and to spy on the military base a few kilometres up the road. The owner of my newspaper, David Cadogan, loved a good story in an English tabloid way; I knew he'd want me to get on board. Besides, I was writing a children's novel, and the trawler would make a good setting for a spy story.

I headed my imitation-wood panelled Ford station wagon towards the wharf and told a local man unloading fish at the bottom of the gangway, "If I'm not off the boat in fifteen minutes, come and look for me."

The Soviet fishermen greeted me with enthusiasm. I was given a grand tour of the trawler's bowels, watched Russians filleting fish with sharp knives, and was escorted, stumbling in the dim light, from one end of the boat to the other, to see inside the huge freezer. (I admit the opening of that heavy door caused me a slight shiver of alarm.) When I finally emerged back on deck, I looked up at the bridge and saw I was being regarded with interest by a couple of men in suits. It was time to leave.

It happened that the military base was where I lived with my husband, Sam, and my children Charles, Katya, and James. Sam, a flight commander, was off on one of his usual missions in an F-101 Voodoo fighter jet to intercept some Russian Bear bomber aircraft off the coast of Newfoundland. After hearing of my escapade he told me that Soviets had been seen on the base trying to sell cigarettes. Certainly high-level tar, but low-level infiltration, I thought. He said the trawler was being keenly watched by the RCMP and warned, "Don't be surprised if you get a call from the Mounties." But I heard nothing. I wrote my story for the newspaper about the experience and finished "Mystery on the Miramichi".

In 1984 we were posted to Germany, near the famous old spa town of Baden-Baden where my husband would be a military intelligence officer for the West at almost the same time as Lieutenant Colonel Vladimir Putin, later Russia's president, held a similar appointment for the KGB in Dresden.

Perhaps they eyed each other across the Wall when Sam was in Berlin for intelligence briefings. One of the western venues was close to the Wall, and there was always extra activity on the eastern side when allied intelligence seekers met for updates and conferences. Sam's demeanour is a bit like Putin's—stern, reserved, and often acerbic when called upon to state his point of view. (A trapped window seat airline passenger might choose to jump over Sam rather than wake him.) Nevertheless, his sense of humour is almost as strong as mine—his stops short of silliness—and, unlike Putin, Sam is tall and built like a hockey player while the Russian is short and wiry like the judo champion he is.

In Germany the family was surrounded by Cold War spy stories, rich material for another novel I had started. At my son James' German public school, the father of one of his classmates had recently been arrested for spying. The man, whom we had probably met at PTA meetings, was charged with stealing the secrets of a British fighter aircraft, the *Tornado*, for the East during the seventies.

My sixteen-year-old son Charles, an outgoing, charming, and quick-witted teenager, was employed on the military base during his summer holidays from boarding school in Canada. He worked for the nuclear and biological unit helping to clean the fallout shelters. These were concrete tubes covered by earth and grass with interiors designed like submarines. Each cigar-shaped mound had a large concrete door at one end that swung open to reveal the decontamination area. The engine room was next with its life-supporting generators, and then the work places. The sleeping area was a series of hammocks slung from the ceiling. Mould grew easily on the damp concrete walls, and it had to be cleaned off to keep the shelters ready for emergency occupation. Their presence was a constant reminder of the climate of the times.

Meanwhile, Sam's job included taking part in training exercises that had him playing a defector from Eastern Europe trying to land his plane at the Canadian base. And one day, while strolling in Baden-Baden with the family, he amused us by hiding in a doorway to avoid coming face to face with a uniformed Russian colonel from the Soviet Union diplomatic military mission in the city. He had a profile and a photograph of the man on his office wall, he explained.

Collecting profiles is a routine job for people in the intelligence business. The more one knows about a person the easier it is to anticipate future actions and exploit flaws. Sam's details would have adorned the walls of the Soviet mission: born in Ottawa, educated at Acadia University and Queen's, light brown hair, hazel eyes, early forties. His profile would also reveal that he had flown on fighter jets that intercepted Russian aircraft. The fact that he had taught mathematics at Royal Military College for a number of years indicated that they were dealing with a more studious individual. His photograph would have shown a resemblance to Brian Mulroney, the Prime Minister of Canada at the time (although we were never quite sure whether it was the jutting chin, aquiline nose, hair, or large head that caused people around the world to comment on this). When Sam eventually met the prime minister face to face, he reported that Mulroney's head was bigger.

In order to gather even more atmosphere for my new book, *Black Forest Secret*, I wanted to see the house that was the official Soviet Union diplomatic military mission to the Baden-Baden area. So I took the kids for a walk. Together with James, who was nine at the time, and Katya, who was fourteen, we got a charge out of seeing the building's barred windows and listening and receiving antennae, and the cars with the number plates especially assigned to the in-country Soviets—the kind we were told to report if seen in the vicinity of the Canadian base.

It was drizzling with rain. As we meandered by, James chose that moment to impersonate John Cleese performing his "German walk" from the BBC television series *Fawlty Towers,* followed by a quick Gene Kelly *Singin' in the Rain* sequence around a lamppost. On this quiet street of stately homes, his outburst of humour was bound to draw attention to us. Sam had warned me that across the road, the French military had their own expensive house in which their spies monitored the electronic and human traffic to and from the Soviet mission, information that they shared with their western allies. Still, we might have gotten away with the "mother and children out for walk" scenario if the street hadn't turned out to be a dead end, forcing us to retrace our steps. Sometime later Sam's French colleagues handed him a photograph of the three of us walking along, looking furtive.

A short while later, Katya accompanied me to East Berlin for a little "look-see" at the other side of the Wall after I managed to join an "educational tour" to Berlin with some teachers from the Canadian base. The attraction was spending the day in the city's east sector. There was one drawback: our two passports were clearly stamped with, "issued to a dependent of a member of the Canadian Armed Forces." I wondered how this would play out with the East German border guards.

All went smoothly until we entered the East Berlin subway station at Griebnitzee to return to West Berlin—Katya was challenged by a guard as not being the person represented in her passport. She had to remove her coat and was questioned by several officials before given permission to leave. Tall, attractive, and affable, I think she secretly enjoyed the drama. But the sight of soldiers with sniffer dogs checking under the train, and unfortunate would-be escapees being escorted from compartments, was sobering. The atmosphere was as suspenseful as it was surreal, but good training for a future secret agent.

After we had been posted back to Ottawa we spent two years in the capital before my husband came home with new, more exciting marching orders in late 1989. He would receive Russian-language training before becoming the air force attaché to the Canadian embassy in Moscow.

All the family approved, intrigued by the possibilities for adventure. The scenario was clear—military attachés posted to the Soviet Union had one major role and that was to report on all matters pertaining to the country's military might. Since the Russians weren't very keen on the idea, this meant spying. Soviet military attachés posted in Canada did the same thing. The rule of the game was simple: Don't get caught.

We were enthusiastic about the new job. The bonus was that I was to receive the same espionage training as Sam, although it was unpaid training for me. For the Canadian government, I would be a cheap partner for his spying missions. I didn't care. What was good for Sam was also going to be good for me.

Becoming my husband's diplomatic teammate in the Soviet Union meant passing muster with the head of Canada's military intelligence. Presumably Sam's credentials were already approved, but I wondered what a background check on me would reveal.

My interview took place on one of the top floors of the National Defence Headquarters, where the highest brass dwelled. I'd come straight from the *Frank* office. Considering that I was dealing with military intelligence, I'd taken a longer route through a shopping mall and checked for a "tail."

My husband sat beside me on a soft leather sofa in the office of Admiral Peter Porter. The chief of military intelligence shook hands before retreating behind his large, clean desk in front of windows that looked out on the city. Porter, in his late forties, was tall and lean with a well-trimmed beard. His white shirt gleamed under his navy blue, gold-braided uniform. He was soft spoken and seemed a bit innocent for a GRU equivalent. The GRU, Russia's huge military intelligence directorate, was and still is its most powerful spy agency. The GRU carried an even heavier espionage load than the KGB—six times the number of agents globally than its civilian counterpart.

The admiral was polite and nice, however, in the Canadian way. We'd heard, from a former naval attaché to Moscow, that he was unmarried but with a "female interest" on the West Coast. That's all I knew about him.

I assumed my "I have been interviewing ministers, royalty, pop stars, and garbage men from around the world since the age of dot" pose and relaxed. I wasn't going to talk about my subscriptions to the pink *Manchester Guardian* weekly, my thoughts about US politics, or my visit with my daughter to East Germany. I thought trouble could arise if I sounded too keen on the job, or intelligent.

Porter began the conversation by saying he understood I was a journalist by profession and this might cause something of a problem.

"Why?" I asked disingenuously

"Because," he said, "what if you came across a situation that would make a really good story, say, for the *Globe and Mail*, but which you should reveal only to military intelligence. Where would your loyalty lie?"

That was easy. Knowing how much the *Globe and Mail* would pay for a tip or a freelance story from Moscow (I had already asked them), I would go with my husband's overseas pay packet. So I answered that I had been a journalist for years while my husband had been in the military and had never revealed any state secrets or disseminated any inside information to any newspaper or magazine without his permission.

The admiral seemed relieved. "I see you write children's books," he continued.

Black Forest Secret, based on my visit to East Berlin, was perking at the publishers. Surely he wouldn't have obtained my four other books and found out that at least one other was about spies? (The others were about pirates, smugglers, and counterfeiters.)

But, before I could say anything, the admiral said, "I collect children's books."

That was a conversation stopper. There was nothing wrong with his remark—except it didn't quite fit the general image of a top military spook.

He said he had a collection of Enid Blyton first editions. Since people of a certain age and background all have old Enid Blytons somewhere in their attics (if their mothers haven't thrown them out), I became very enthusiastic. We chatted for a bit about the Famous Five adventures. Of course he also had Arthur Ransom's Swallows and Amazons series and said he had a crow's nest with a telescope at the bottom of his garden on the Rideau River that was like the one Titty and Peggy used. Sam had lost interest in the small talk and only vaguely heard what we were discussing. His only worry, he said later, was that I might get carried away by saying that I too had first editions, a "reporter's white lie."

Then the head of intelligence said he also collected clocks. Ah, what did I know about clocks? A good journalist knows a little about everything … But I caught a warning look in Sam's eyes, which said, "Forget it." The conversation petered out. The interview was over.

The admiral hadn't asked me about *Frank*, and I didn't mention it. I was presented as a perfectly charming, dedicated military wife in her forties, mother of three children. That's what he saw and that's what he could understand. It wouldn't have taken much of a background check to reveal I was a pinkish cynical hack with a penchant for spy novels, an alarming sense of the absurd, and a wild imagination. I returned to my office via another route.

2
Spy School

One just doesn't pack up the house and children and take off for Moscow as a spy. No, there's essential training that turns friendly Canadians into paranoid, Russian-speaking intelligence gatherers.

Most of the returning military attachés from Communist countries found themselves doing jobs in intelligence on the very top floors of the headquarters in Ottawa. You could always tell who they were. They had twitches, they were always looking over their shoulders, they were taking Russian language courses as a hobby, and if you sat next to them on buses and said a friendly "hi," they'd move to another seat. They were suffering from something like shell shock. Or was it the shock of being back in Canada and realizing how much they'd enjoyed the work and the people over on the "other side"? There was one returnee I felt could easily have been a double agent. There certainly weren't too many with a sense of humour so I was careful.

All the new Canadian attachés chosen for postings at embassies around the world were invited to defence headquarters for a meeting. Although most of us were to take language training, only those going to the Soviet Union and Warsaw Pact countries would be learning the essential tools of the military intelligence trade. In

1990 the Soviet Union was intact, and there was no reason to believe it would change. Our training would include how to take covert photographs of surface-to-air missiles (SAM) from fast-moving cars while being dogged by zealous GRU or KGB agents, and how to identify every piece of Soviet weaponry imaginable in order to look for changes in numbers or physical appearance. Our field training was to take place in Ontario, Quebec, and across the border in the United States. I was perfectly willing to subject myself to the training in order to achieve my goal of experiencing the life of an espionage agent abroad.

Talk to me about having to learn French, and an enormous tiredness comes over me. All my life it seems I have been learning French, and I still don't speak the language. Ah, but Russian! The language of the KGB, Moscow Centre, Le Carré … and at the very end of the course a spy job in the Soviet Union for three or four years. Who wouldn't be enthusiastic?

We started our training for Moscow in August 1990 at the dark brown brick Canadian Forces Language School just off the Ottawa Queensway. Next door was a building I suspected was being used by the Canadian Security Intelligence Service (CSIS) for their covert operations. How else to explain why the building's inhabitants changed clothing and cars several times each day? Their location was good—close to an establishment occupied by the military. CSIS had forgotten that spies in training have heightened powers of perception. At least I did. Off people would go on their missions of great national importance, wearing suits one minute and baseball caps the next. Sam shrugged it off as new job paranoia and suggested I stop looking outside during class.

Military attachés at the school were learning Czech, Chinese, Turkish, and Italian. All were accompanied by their wives. After taking many courses during their careers with military colleagues, this sudden spousal togetherness added another dimension to learning for these senior officers.

Sam was the only attaché going to Russia so there were only two of us in class. The lessons lasted six hours a day. During breaks for coffee and lunch, all of us shared a small kitchen where we ate sandwiches, made tea or coffee, used the microwave, and chatted. It was safe to talk about our future posting with the others. Military intelligence officials had told us that in the beginning we were to remain fairly incognito: we weren't supposed to go around broadcasting our appointment to all and sundry because officials in the receiving country didn't know about us yet. Or so we were told. And of course we might fail our training and then any blathering would be embarrassing.

In the classroom we became very competitive. Or at least I did, complaining if Sam got ahead of me by a page or two. With his deep voice, a Russian accent came easily to him. I just twisted the words to suit my mincing southern England vowels. I stored up in my memory any words that came hard to him, like "Munich" (pronounced with a cow-like "Moo," it always gave me a laugh), and used them in class during "questioning one's partner" time. Making him repeat them back to me was my revenge. Annoyingly, he remained completely unaffected. It made me study even harder, and almost every night and every weekend we hit the books.

Several Russian teachers taught at the school. All were about the same age and from the same background—Jewish émigrés from the seventies. Our teacher, Oleg, had been educated at Leningrad University. He limped, the result of falling off his bicycle when he was thirteen and suffering a broken leg that hadn't been set properly. He'd been orphaned during the siege of Leningrad, and he warned us at the start of the course that he was unpredictable and lacked certain social graces because he had been brought up in a Soviet orphanage. Why was he telling us this, we wondered. He controlled his unpredictable streak, he said, by not drinking coffee or tea. Instead, he filled his big Russian teacup with warm milk and water.

We would be together for nine months and a bond sprang up between us, possibly because he was the first Russian we got to know well. We learned the alphabet, then grammar and short sentences. We felt we were getting on terribly well. Then something straight out of a KGB manual began to affect our studies.

The military language school was laying off its permanent teachers and replacing them with contractual instructors. This staffing change saved them money on wages, pensions, and social benefits. It happens everywhere. Oleg had taught at the school for more than ten years and had another four to go before he turned sixty and drew a pension. But the school administration was in a hurry and had targeted him. He would be encouraged to leave, thus forfeiting his benefits. How to accomplish this? By firing him for incompetent teaching and an unsuitable temperament.

It all began in October, about two months into our training. Russian is a tough language to learn, especially if one has reached a certain age and the brain cells are disintegrating, but we were feeling really good the day an administrator sat in on one of our classes. She was to monitor the class and write a report. We swung into action—reading, repeating, writing, speaking, asking and answering questions—in our newly acquired language. We gave a stellar performance, having practised for this eventuality and learned a nice, neat little presentation designed to impress.

The following week a quietly grim Oleg walked into the classroom. At first he wouldn't say what was wrong. He wasn't allowed to tell us, he explained. But he capitulated under a pair of professional grillers and revealed that he'd received his classroom report back from the evaluator. Let's see it, we demanded. No, he said, I'm not allowed to involve students. Rubbish, we told him. He finally handed us the report, and we were stunned. What we read bore no resemblance at all to what had gone on in the classroom. It was just a diatribe about Oleg's abilities and could have been written any time, any place. How would our performance as students be evaluated if we were supposed to have such a bad teacher?

Things got worse over the next month or so. We had to hand in our textbooks because the school wanted us to use different ones. Oleg ordered new Russian textbooks, but they didn't arrive. Instead manuals arrived that he had never seen before, and he was told to teach from them. Oleg managed to obtain copies of the books he knew well from another source and gave them to us wrapped in brown paper. Since the door was now being opened frequently by administrative staff "looking in," he pleaded with us to hide them quickly under the desk. Was this Ottawa or Moscow? Perhaps it was all part of our training. Were we passing or failing?

Learning Russian had become an uphill battle, but it strengthened our resolve to try even harder. The toll on Oleg, however, was inevitable. Here was a man who had escaped from the Soviet Union. After spending some time in a refugee camp in Italy, he had finally succeeded in coming to Canada, the land of fair play. Now this. The pressure built. In January, at a staff meeting with administration, he finally broke. He banged his hand on the table, shouted, and lashed out with his foot. He was suspended without pay. We had a new teacher.

Fortunately, unions don't like this kind of thing happening to their members. The Department of National Defence (DND) was taken to court by the Public Service Union on Oleg's behalf. Sam was called as a witness for Oleg. On the opposing side was the commandant, an officer of equal rank.

The attachés in the sandwich room were divided on whether we should have participated. At least two of them were of the opinion that if I hadn't been in the classroom encouraging Sam, he wouldn't have got involved in his teacher's fight in the first place. But we were satisfied. Oleg was reinstated as our teacher and went on to retire at the age of sixty with his pension.

As we approached the final semester following the Easter break in 1991 and were by now surely on our way to Russia, the door of the classroom suddenly burst open, and in came a camera crew and interviewer Andrei Filatov from Radio Moscow. A young non-commissioned officer (NCO) from the school was with them. Filatov, a smooth-talking, dark-haired, good-looking Russian, spoke fluent English and quickly asked us our names and whether we were looking forward to going to Moscow. Oleg sunk white faced below his desk. My husband told the reporter and crew to get the hell out of the classroom, lambasted the escorting officer, and later complained to the commandant. Oleg, the Jewish émigré, had recognized the group for what they were—only KGB-approved Russian journalists were allowed to live and work outside the Soviet Union—and he did not want to be filmed by them teaching military attachés.

So much for being discreet about our posting before the host country had officially sanctioned it. Since secrecy and diplomacy had been preached from day one, it seemed ridiculous for the school to be aiding the real KGB to meet prospective spies before we'd even set foot in Moscow.

But it wasn't the commandant's fault. The visit must have been approved at a much higher level. We didn't know it then but we were bit players in a small, unfolding Cold War melodrama.

As we watched the Radio Moscow team drive away from the school in an unmarked blue van, Oleg told us that part of his fear and surprise had come from the fact he'd already met the brash interviewer. Despite his game leg and age, Oleg regularly exercised by running alongside the Ottawa River. A few days earlier he had encountered a man and a woman standing on the footpath talking in Russian. The woman was blond and very beautiful. The man was Filatov. Oleg had to go around them, but as he did the couple said something to him in Russian, and he stopped. Oleg told us he'd chatted for a bit and then taken off. They hadn't been around when he returned. Was it a chance meeting? He didn't know and was spooked.

As it happened, it wasn't a chance meeting. The Russian broadcaster was making overtures to defect. Approaching the language school to do an interview with prospective military attachés gave him the right contacts. It also provided an excellent cover if his own people were watching him, and any interview would have been regarded by the KGB as a scoop.

He defected later to a major I happened to know in Public Affairs in the DND, an affable person who wouldn't know a good guy from a bad one. In an intricate arrangement, Filatov and his wife set off in their car after dark to a secret meeting place in Ottawa. Waiting for them there were all the usual suspects as well as the public affairs officer. There was much switching on and off of headlights and excitement until the Russian couple decided it was all clear and changed vehicles and countries.

His blond wife was the daughter of a KGB general. Later, I also heard from one of my Russian journalist sources that she had worked as a secretary for the American Ambassador in Moscow before coming to Canada. I saw the very attractive Russian couple eating at an expensive Ottawa restaurant a few years later. I heard Filatov had been given a job with CBC Radio in Montreal. He was probably broadcasting back to Russia.

Despite all the distractions at the language school, we learned as much Russian as we could, passed the required tests, and graduated. But we were only halfway there. It was all the "other Secret Agent 101" training that was to turn us into Double O Sevens.

3

Working with Spooks

Our spy craft training was conducted in the windowless basement of a building in Ottawa. It ran simultaneously with language studies so we had to take days off from Oleg's class to attend these meetings. Our absences must have added to his frustration, but he had been teaching attachés for years and knew the routine. At other times our practical training occupied our weekends and holidays.

Because it was an ultrasecret area, we needed special passes to go downstairs each time we visited the basement, and even then we were escorted. The experts who would tell us where to go when we were "in country" and what to look for worked here.

Eastern spies would have loved the place. It was where our spooks studied satellite imagery of the Communist world as well as the latest photographs taken by military attachés—sent out of foreign embassies via the diplomatic bag. The latter, which doesn't have to be a bag but can be any container from the embassy marked "diplomatic," has immunity and, according to international convention, can't be opened or detained by the host nation. The couriers who accompany the mail also have special status under the 1961 Vienna Convention.

During training, we never learned how to shoot real bullets. I was disappointed because I thought I would be a good shot. I was good at throwing things accurately—darts, cricket balls, horseshoes, objects into wastepaper baskets—but I could see our trainers' reasoning. You can rip out your film and expose it, you can eat your rice paper notes, but it's awfully difficult to hide a gun. There's also the temptation to use it if manhandled by the enemy. "Military wife shoots border guard to protect husband" would not be a headline the Canadian government would welcome.

We had to be able to identify all of the Soviet Union's weaponry, and once again I was a dedicated student. Never mind that it amounted to hundreds of guns, cannons, artillery, grenade throwers, missile and rocket launchers, trucks, jeeps, armoured personnel carriers, tanks, mine layers, mine detectors, command vehicles, airplanes, helicopters, ships, and submarines dating back to the Second World War. We listened to the sound of the weaponry until we knew the difference between an oncoming T55 and a T80 tank. We watched films of Soviet bombers and helicopters, and could identify in an instant a MiG-29 or Su-27 fighter jet from brief video clips or obscure photographs. I whisked through flashcards as I made supper. Nuclear rockets were easy. When I scored my final pass mark of 75 per cent (apparently not bad for someone off the street or a wife), I knew it was another step towards my life as a spy. I could pick up the other 25 per cent on the job.

I managed to inject a little fun into the sessions by asking dumb questions such as, "Why do tanks have muzzle brakes? To stop shells from leaving the muzzle at the last minute if you happen to change your mind?" But on the whole I kept my humour in check and behaved very well because I wanted to learn as much as possible. The more I knew, the better I would be able to perform my role in Moscow.

Weaponry wasn't the only thing we had to identify. Antennae have never looked the same to me: the nodding ones, the banana-shaped ones, and the antennae that told me, watch out, there's a

SAM base nearby. I still look at them to this day.

Working with spooks must be like working with psychiatrists—always eyeing you as if whatever you have said or done is a little suspicious, never quite normal. I shelved my habit, unconsciously developed over the years, of scanning every exposed piece of paper, upside down or otherwise, left on desks. My husband had drawn my attention to the habit when I visited his office. In this basement I tried to keep my eyes firmly off others' property and only read the documents I was given in our assigned office. There would be a time and place later for sneakiness.

Although my husband was in the armed forces, it was my father who had instilled in me an interest in things military. I was born in Aldershot, England, which for countless years—even during Roman times—had been known for its huge army camp. When I was a child my father took me to watch British soldiers, bands, tanks, and guns whenever they paraded through the town's streets. We waved and cheered because "we'd won the war."

He wasn't in the military, except for a four-year stint in the air force during the war, but his father had been a permanent member. He died when my father was only four or five. As a child my father had sat on a grassy knoll above Aldershot Station and watched as train after train disgorged the First World War wounded, dead, and dying from France. Despite these early gory scenes, he became a military buff.

Just down the road from Aldershot is Farnborough, the site of the international air show. Every year the whole family packed a picnic and attended the flying displays. One year a jet fighter disintegrated over a hill of spectators, killing several, the end of the exciting "fly over the crowd and thrill 'em" era. It was usually our viewing spot, but fortunately we were picnicking on another part of the grounds that day. We saw the Armstrong Whitworth "flying wing" at Farnborough, and the Bristol Brabazon—at the time one of the largest aircraft in the world—lift off over our heads, almost bowling us over. As for ships, my father and I toured HMS *Indefatigable* when she was in Portsmouth, and I rode up and down on the airplane lift.

Tanks, planes, and ships: if they were on display, my father was there with me in tow, and I suppose I inherited some of his curiosity about things military. A lot of the Russian weaponry we studied was from my father's generation. The added attraction was the excitement of thinking we were being shown "for your eyes only" stuff.

Two men from military intelligence were assigned to teach us weaponry identification and spy photography. Their main task, however, was to create and organize realistic and frightening scenarios for our benefit, in southern Ontario and parts of Quebec. These situations were meant to be the kind that could occur to military attachés going about their business in the Soviet Union and would test our suitability and enthusiasm for the job.

Our two handlers were in their mid-fifties. One was a civilian, Laurie Dean, while the other was an army master warrant officer, Dale Sinclair. A droll, divorced Englishman of medium height, with a thin, florid face under wispy grey hair and rimless reading glasses, Dean always wore a tie with dark suits or a blazer and favoured blue shirts. On chilly days I saw him crossing the parking lot in a heavy, belted navy-blue raincoat. He sat at one end of the table while his colleague, who typically wore a dark-green, army-issue sweater over his uniform shirt and trousers, sat at the other. Sinclair had a brush cut and wore owlish, heavy-framed glasses. He told us he was coming up for retirement soon. I could make him quite jolly just by smiling at him, as if he was relieved that I didn't hate the course. Dean was more businesslike than Sinclair.

Joining the four of us were Bill and Mary Jones, a couple going to Czechoslovakia (now the Czech Republic). Jones, an army colonel, had thinning, peppery brown hair and a large, round face with watery hazel eyes. He wore glasses too and was forever pushing them up his shiny nose. The attachés wore their uniforms to work because the basement and the language school were in military establishments. Jones' wife was rather glamorous. She wore her wavy light brown hair caught up at the back in a comb, bright lipstick, and dresses that revealed her cleavage.

The photography course was interesting. I'd been using a camera for years professionally and prided myself on having a good journalistic eye, but this was different. Passing a SAM site in a car, a spy can't slow down, pause, and then take a photo. No, a spy has to learn how to take a good, clean shot from a fast-moving vehicle. Never mind if the sun is not over one's left shoulder. A spy has to learn how to snap the inside of a building when the door is ajar but the contents are in darkness and how to catch moving tanks, columns of troops, and the underbellies, intakes, and cockpits of aircraft. Then there are the long-distance photos of aircraft carriers in port and the manoeuvres of the latest fighter.

From our first day of spy craft in the fall of 1990, we were given 35-mm cameras with various lenses with which to practise. We were encouraged to shoot everything everywhere in Ottawa, including the tanks inside the military museum. At a sports day at his boarding school in Port Hope, Ontario, my son James, then fourteen, was embarrassed to have both a father and a mother so well endowed with cameras and equipment. I found the long-distance lenses the most cumbersome and heavy. Weighing only 105 pounds, I kept falling on my face. Not a good sign.

We used our cameras constantly during the practical training. The latter, devised by Dean and Sinclair and doled out in increasingly heavy doses during our course, was a time for the Canadian military police and Special Investigation Unit, the RCMP, customs officers, CSIS, and CSE to pretend they were KGB and use detention, intimidation, physical threats, and coercion to test our fortitude and to try to prevent us from "spying." We were about to be subjected to some serious KGB-style tactics. I was confident we would prove to be ideal spy candidates.

We'd been told that we would have pretend KGB minders with us throughout the year in Ottawa. They would go through our garbage looking for incriminating material like bank statements, credit card receipts, old cheques, and letters. We would be filmed, photographed, and followed. We couldn't take anything for granted, and we had to be ready for anything. It was brainwashing in the sense that I am still not comfortable with throwing personal information into the household garbage, I automatically check the source of the camera when flashes go off in public places, and if I pass the same stranger more than twice while out shopping I feel uneasy.

On our first on-the-road trip as trainee spies during September 1989, we travelled to Carp, an area outside of Ottawa, where the government maintained a giant bomb shelter (now a museum). En route to the town, a middle-aged couple passed us in a large sedan. As we approached the town, we saw them come out of a store, look at us, and hurry towards their vehicle as if they hadn't expected us so early. Perhaps they were new as well.

We stopped at a restaurant for a coffee. Everything appeared normal. Just as we were leaving, a waitress approached us and said, "You dropped this." It was someone's credit card. Sam took it. Outside the restaurant two men were waiting for us. They wanted to know what documents we had taken from the woman and why. Sam had been successfully trapped. The waitress was part of the game. We had failed the "don't take anything from strangers" rule. One of the men put his hands on Sam's arm. "Don't touch me, I'm a diplomat," he said, getting into the spirit of things. Finally we were allowed to get into our car. We followed the prescribed route home and took a few photographs of antennae.

The second trip took us to Kingston, Ontario in October. On that occasion, we were driving a car with red diplomatic plates just as we would in Moscow. We stayed at a Holiday Inn near the wharf. Even then we were wary of talking in our room. Sam looked carefully out the window. I undressed for bed in the bathroom. We heard some comings and goings on the floor but nothing abnormal. The next day we were escorted to the room next door for a show-and-tell session. Our room was full of bugging devices. Our minders had been able to listen to us, see us, and even had a photo of my husband peeking out the curtain. This is what will happen to you every day in the Soviet Union, we were told by a Canadian intelligence technician. We were undaunted and nodded nonchalantly.

Leaving the hotel, we found our car with a flat tire, sitting forlornly in the parking lot. We asked the hotel manager if he had a tire pump. Funny you should ask, he said. For the past three years, cars that have stopped here with red diplomatic plates invariably end up with flat tires. So he had finally bought a pump. Before heading back to Ottawa, we stopped at the wharf to take a few photographs. As we were walking back, a car drove quickly towards us and stopped, blocking our path. "Never leave a distance between yourselves and your exit vehicle," said the driver.

We were learning not to take anyone for granted and to be ready for the unexpected. The feeling of being watched crept into our everyday life, and we checked around us before stepping into and out of the car, our house, neighbourhood stores, and restaurants. Our training was on track.

After each trip we were debriefed back in the Ottawa basement, and Dean critiqued us on our behaviour. Clothing was an issue. Light-coloured jackets were out, especially yellow ones. It was also better to be a brunette rather than a blond or a redhead. So I was okay. Pointing, as in "do you see who I see" or "that's our target," was also frowned upon. I think Dean was challenged by our enjoyment and enthusiasm, perhaps mistaking these qualities for a smarty-pants attitude.

What we had encountered so far was mild. Even when Sam and I flew down to Hamilton, Ontario a month later on board a small aircraft that was supposed to feel like Aeroflot, we weren't too apprehensive and assumed that among our fellow passengers were federal intelligence agents following us like the real KGB would do on flights within the Soviet Union. It didn't take much imagination (and I have plenty) to make the scenario feel real, but the sense of danger wasn't there—yet!

The next mission, to a place just outside of Kingston, Ontario near Point Petrie in February 1991 tested our mettle and offered a heavy dose of realism. We were accompanied on this trip by an air force sergeant, Terry Meader, who was going to work in the Moscow embassy office as an intelligence NCO. He needed some training as well and drove on the first leg of our trip. Meader was about forty and his wife and two young children would be accompanying him to Moscow. He had a bright face and was cheerful and animated.

We'd been given a topographical map with a marked target of a radar tower at Point Petrie. Sam sat in the front passenger seat. I was by myself in the back. The route took us off the road and through bushes and trees down a very long and rough dirt track to a grass clearing. What was supposed to be a tower turned out to be some abandoned buildings. It was quiet, too quiet. There was only one way in and one way out. We photographed the buildings anyway and were driving back down the track when a black van approached ominously.

The vehicle swerved into our path and stopped. We halted. There was nowhere to go anyway. The doors opened and four hooded and masked men jumped out carrying machine guns. They wore camouflage trousers tucked into heavy black army boots and strode purposefully over to our car. From either side of the vehicle they screamed at Meader to wind down his window. He wound it down a little and the muzzle of a machine gun was jammed into the crack.

A "KGB guard" barked at us, "Who are you? What are you doing here? This is private property." We didn't reply. The muzzle of the gun twisted towards me in the back seat. He signalled to the other armed men, and they went to the van, pulled out a very large, heavy tarpaulin and proceeded to cover our vehicle. We were left sitting in semidarkness. The gun remained in place. Knowing that this was supposed to be a game wasn't necessarily comforting. Outside were four heavily armed people. Their adrenalin, like ours, was running high. Did they all know this was a game, or had a few details been left out to make them behave more realistically? We didn't know how long we would be under the tarpaulin but one of us found a flashlight, and we decided it was a good time to eat our cheese sandwiches.

Suddenly the tarpaulin was lifted on the driver's side, and Meader was told to get out of the vehicle or he would be shot. He was "helped" out and thrust to the ground. We could see him lying face down beside the car, his beard pressed into mud and decaying grass, and his hands tied behind his back. He was protesting, "I am a diplomat," as we had been taught. He had thrown us a wry smile as he was dragged from the vehicle, but now his cheerfulness had left him, and his voice sounded worried. He was not enjoying the treatment.

We thought it was our turn next, and I was debating whether I would go along with the game or kick someone in the groin. But no, they concentrated on poor Meader and pushed him into the back of the truck for "interrogation." Two other guns remained pointed at us. I wondered what would happen if a family of picnickers wandered down this scenic path towards Lake Ontario. Masked men holding hostages would be an interesting sight.

The same thought might have entered our captors' heads because as quickly as it had started the incident was over. The tarpaulin was taken off, the NCO was released, and the men took off in a hurry in their van. After a few deep breaths and brave smiles all round, we followed. There was no sign of our assailants.

We remained calm but cautious until we reached the main road. Then driving back to Ottawa we compared notes on the incident. Because the car was a rental and probably bugged, we calmed the excited sergeant and kept most of our own chatter for later when we were safely inside the house. Our response to the harassment had been appropriately cool, we thought, but we were a rare group. Some trainees became very upset by this kind of treatment, judging by remarks made by our language school colleagues.

It was clear that from now on the gloves were off. How far would Dale and Sinclair push us? No matter, Sam and I were out to prove ourselves and to try and beat the opposing forces. We laughed about it and agreed it was a crazy way to make a living, but more fun than a desk job.

On our next outing, from Montreal and Quebec City to Bagotville, where there was a Canadian Forces base, we were travelling with the Joneses, the couple going to Czechoslovakia. They were uptight about the training, although we didn't realize it at first. We were prepared for the worst kind of scenario but had a gung-ho approach. I think their attitude was more normal.

The hotels were carefully chosen to resemble Soviet ones. There were no star listings. It was March 1991, and the weather still cold when we set off from the seedy Montreal hotel in a rented car following a prescribed route down a wide boulevard. But Bill Jones, who was driving, had been brought up in Montreal and, excited we were passing the area of his boyhood home, decided to take a look. One moment we were travelling west, the next we'd made a U-turn and were travelling east, then north, then west again. He was pointing out his house, and we were turning down small roads. Consequently we lost all of our followers until we reached Quebec City. He may have done it on purpose, reluctant to encounter any of Dale and Sinclair's hair-raising scenarios. Perhaps a milder training program was okay for him—he was going to Prague where the political climate had warmed—but not for us. We wanted to experience Ottawa's version of the heavy-handed tactics of a still chilly security service, although with some trepidation now because any script changes caused by our manoeuvrings would stir our comrades to even more sadistic behaviour.

We booked into another low-class motel near Quebec City, and all was quiet until we were departing the next morning. Mary and I got into the back of the car as we waited for the men to pay the bill, and we carefully locked the car doors. We were chatting when a man ran up to the car and tried the door handle on the driver's side. Thankfully he couldn't get in and ran off. But our relief was short-lived. We heard running footsteps. The man had acquired master keys! He leapt into the car, turned on the ignition, and we were off. Now was this part of the game, or were we being hijacked by a disturbed car thief?

My companion in the back seat, not wanting to find out whose hands we were in, opened her door to get out. We were accelerating into the fast lane of a highway, the driver's blood was at boiling point, and a female passenger was about to slide out into the traffic. I shouted, "No, don't," and grabbed Mary's arm. I yelled at the driver to stop. He was concentrating on the traffic, but I shook his shoulder. Fortunately he looked in the mirror. The corporal or sergeant realized instantly that killing a colonel's wife in the middle of a highway was not a good idea, game or no game. No, it would be a serious public relations problem. He slowed. We got Mary in and calmed down and returned to the motel where Sam and Bill, mystified by our disappearance, waited. When they saw who our driver was, they knew that we had all been caught napping by Dean and Co.

Then we set off once more towards our target, this time in a more normal fashion.

Sam was driving now. He kept an eye on the car behind and was fascinated at the way it could change its headlights at will. Sometimes the right headlight was on, sometimes just the left, other times both of them. It would have been very confusing at night but an effective cover. The driver was a youngish woman. She had a male companion. We came over the brow of the hill and saw a small café on the right and decided we all needed a coffee. The other car would have shot by if the passenger hadn't caught sight of our brake lights. It did a sharp U-turn and followed us into the parking lot. Then another car turned in and yet another. Eight of us went into the restaurant. A few others hovered outside. The woman who had been driving behind us spoke to us and told us how bad we'd been the previous day when we'd lost them in Montreal. And we hadn't behaved very well during the morning kidnapping, either. Then they left.

We were just getting into our car to hit the road again when Sam had a thought. Suppose that encounter had just been a distraction, suppose ... Remembering the words of Laurie Dean in Ottawa, "Ignore the overt operatives, it's the covert ones you have to worry about," he ran to the back of the car and looked underneath. Sure enough, while we were drinking coffee and chatting, a homing device the size of an apple had been planted there. He ripped it off and threw it into the trunk. We too could make a game of this. (It was a piece of expensive equipment that had been signed out by the "KGB" crew, and they apparently became very worried when it stopped working. "It could have been a bomb, you should have left it alone," we were told during a later debriefing.)

Another very cheap motel was our designated stop in Chicoutimi. We felt vulnerable, expecting an encounter of some kind, but nothing happened. Jones drove the next day, and our route was supposed to take us across the Saguenay River, past the Canadian Forces Base at Bagotville, through a national park area, and back towards Quebec City. But the army attaché had already resolved not to go anywhere near the base. He said he knew a shortcut that would exclude the military establishment but not take us too far off our official route. Something was waiting on that base that the Joneses did not want to know about. And this was only an exercise.

I was disappointed because I wanted to experience everything Dale and Co. could throw at us. As it turned out, during our spy life in the former Soviet Union, we needed to be able to cope with everything in the book.

What Jones failed to realize was that by pulling the homing device off the car and then bypassing the military base, we had again made our "friends" very upset. We were not obeying their rules, and they thought we needed to be taught a lesson.

We were heading along the highway that follows the Saguenay River through a national park when we first saw the helicopter—a small, brown light Huey. For the next few kilometres it was like being in a James Bond movie. The helicopter chased our car, buzzing and circling it. It rose up out of a valley on our left and hovered menacingly over us. Then it sank over hills on our right, reappearing minutes later, heading straight for us. As this was a highway on which normal traffic was travelling, I've no idea how dangerously entertaining this show was for the other drivers. Bill was white and sweating. But he couldn't watch the helicopter as closely as we could. He had to keep his eyes on the road. He just heard our "Here it comes again" as it clattered noisily over us.

We were surprised at the ease with which the helicopter found us each time, among many similar cars on the road. We found out afterwards that our minders had taped a white cross on the roof of the vehicle while we'd been asleep in our Chicoutimi motel.

A radar site we were supposed to photograph was coming up rapidly on our right. Sam was navigating and was surprised when Jones overshot the site. "We have to go back," demanded my husband. He's a perfectionist, and I'm a control freak, so we were doomed not to miss this one. Reluctant and shaken, Bill pulled onto the shoulder and when it was safe made a 180-degree turn. Sweat had broken out on his forehead. His glasses had slipped to the end of his nose. "There it is," said my husband, pointing at a muddy gravel road to our left. We drove in, taking photographs as we went, and the small road quickly became a dirt track. We travelled a short way into the woods and stopped the car in a large clearing.

Of course it was a trap, but this was training: one frightening scenario after another so that we'd become immune to guns, masked men, and intimidation.

No sooner had we stopped than the helicopter swooped in. Masked men carrying machine guns descended on ropes. It was the same routine as with the tarpaulin, but the people were nastier and meaner, and we were in semidarkness much longer. It was a good opportunity to rip the film from our cameras and used spools, and eat our rice paper notes and directions. In another country we might have more to worry about than just getting lead poisoning. Eventually, the cover was lifted and the guns were pointed at us all. I hoped they weren't playing with real ammunition. Both attachés insisted they were diplomats and couldn't be treated in "this threatening manner."

"Are you ready to come out and confess?" they screamed at us in response.

I have to admit I was probably a little apprehensive at times. The trainers really got into their roles, and they were playing with guns. You could look at the masked attackers and think they were just play-acting, but there was no winking or nodding or friendliness about them. But I was always able to tell myself, "This will be terrific material for future use." And now, after living for more than fifteen years on and off in Russia and other parts of the former Soviet Union, I've become pretty blasé about this kind of activity.

It seemed like hours before our captors finally released us, and we backed out onto the highway and sped off. We stayed another night in Quebec City. The next morning Bill wanted to drive again. Sam was obviously too keen for his liking. But no, we insisted, and drove back to Montreal to catch our flight to Ottawa. The only incident occurred on the highway when we were boxed in by three cars and forced onto the hard shoulder. There was a Greyhound bus behind us, and the driver and his passengers went by with their mouths agape. But no sooner had he passed than our followers took off and disappeared down the highway. They were just demonstrating how easy it is to trap someone.

That manoeuvre would have been a lot more difficult for them after our terrorist driving course at Ottawa International Airport. All the attachés and their spouses gathered for the course, which was taught by two instructors in two large American sedans. We were divided into two groups, no husbands and wives together. Then for two days using a deserted runway we learned high-speed defensive driving around pylons and through obstacle courses. We learned how, at 120 kilometres per hour, to jump lanes suddenly without swerving or losing control and do 180-degree turns, both forwards and backwards, with rubber flying into the open car windows until we were covered with the black stuff. We wore out two sets of tires in two days. I remember steaming backwards down the runway, building power to do my 180, when I looked over my shoulder and saw the faces of the two male attachés in the back seat. The sight of their fear broke me up with laughter, and I barely had the strength to complete the wheel turn.

After the course we were told to go home and relax and not drive that evening. Apparently one trainee had gone straight from a course to test-drive a car he was buying from a dealership. The car salesman barely survived the spin along the Queensway while the attaché, still on a high, demonstrated all his newfound skills.

Meanwhile, there were other things to do to prepare for Moscow, including having my fingerprints taken. Was this to identify my dead body later? Fingerprinting would seem like quite a straightforward task, but it's amazing how much stress my fingers had been subjected to over the years from writing, typing, cooking, cleaning (with the usual hazardous substances), burning (on hot stoves), and cutting (with paring knives). It seems I barely had any prints left. So the special investigation unit or was it the military police—they all began to blend into one—appointed a woman to kneel on my fingers as an impression was taken. I think I failed the exercise. I was the "spy without identifiable prints." And when you are dealing with intelligence services in any country, this is not a bad thing.

We had one more operation to go before we were declared fit, or paranoid enough, to embark on our spying mission. We knew we had probably reached the appropriate paranoia level when we were out for a pleasant stroll on a Sunday afternoon, and a van stopped beside us. The driver leaned across the passenger seat and asked for directions to an antique dealer on the other side of the Ottawa River in Quebec. Our hair prickled. We tersely gave him directions to the nearest bridge. He didn't seem in a hurry to leave. "I'm an antique dealer from Sarnia," he said. That was the hometown of Sam's father. We were being tested. He asked us if we were interested in Ontario antiques, he had some brochures ... "No, no thanks," we said, walking off quickly before he could give us anything that slightly resembled a document. Feeling proud of ourselves, we reported the incident to our handler in the basement. "Don't know anything about it," he said. "It wasn't us. Perhaps it was the other side. Look out for them. They know you are going to Moscow and they might not be able to resist approaching you."

Our final mission took us over the International Bridge at Prescott, Ontario and into the United States. Again we were with Mary and Bill Jones, but this time we were in two cars. Bill drove his car, while we had a rental. After reaching New York State, we followed the St. Lawrence River west. We were supposed to re-enter Canada at the Cornwall crossing. Anything could have been planned between the two borders, and we felt sure the trip was going to be eventful.

Our first excitement came at a roadblock set up by the New York State Troopers. Since Canadian and American spies worked closely together in Moscow during the Cold War, it wasn't hard to assume that the New York State Police were part of the set-up. There was a lineup of traffic, but when they got to us the troopers didn't seem overly excited or interested. Just routine, they said. They were looking for some escaped prisoners. Could they inspect our trunk? Sure, we agreed. It only took a few moments, and we were on our way. The other two, up ahead, had got through the roadblock just as fast and easily as we had.

Of course after we left, the troopers had probably telephoned the approaching Cornwall customs crossing to say, "The suckers are on their way."

There were certain antennae and buildings we had to photograph as we rode along. I had the film out of the camera and safely in my pocket when we swung towards the border. We had reached the Canadian side when we were pulled over by customs officials. The Joneses' car had already come to a halt ahead of us. "Get out." We reached for our bags with our cameras and passports. By that time we'd also been issued with very small cameras for photographing documents.

The men were immediately placed up against the side of the cars with their hands behind their heads and searched. It was very realistic, serious, and rough. I hoped the customs guys had been let in on the secret. I could see Jones getting uncomfortable. His wife was too. All this was taking place in front of cars passing through the border. Tough customs officers in Canada, eh?

Jones remembered he had left his bag in his car. He wanted to retrieve it, but the more he tried to move towards the vehicle, the more he was restrained. "We'll get the bag," a customs officer said. Yes, it was an exercise, but they were going to give a good performance. We hoped they knew when to stop so we would learn exactly what it feels like to be apprehended as a spy or terrorist without getting into too much trouble. My heart was pounding as I waited for their next move, but it was more from excitement than the fear a real suspect might feel. I could play-act too: I was an international spy who wasn't about to give up her film of secret installations easily.

We were marched into the customs building. The police took the

Joneses away and left us sitting in a small interrogation room with a few chairs and a table. I had the foresight to look under the table and discovered something that I, being a fan of the spy genre, had always wanted to see: a voice-activated tape recorder fixed to the underside. I motioned to my husband not to say anything unless it was something he wanted the police to hear. (I still look under tables in restaurants just hoping to recapture that initial excitement of spotting something. But now listeners can use cellphones lying on tabletops to broadcast conversations to the world, and there are many more sophisticated bugging devices.)

After a wait of about fifteen minutes, we were taken to a larger room down the hall where the customs' chief and another uniformed officer sat. We looked around the room and knew we were being both filmed and recorded. Let's do well on this, we both thought. The chief lounged back in his chair as if he was ready to enjoy the show. He also intended to put on a good performance.

We were asked to remove our winter coats. Fortunately I had already transferred the film to my trouser pocket and was determined not to give it up, although I wouldn't have said "over my dead body." There was a brief struggle when Sam refused to give up our attaché bag, but he was overpowered by the two men. They started to go through the bag, pulling out cameras, rice paper, and spare film. We protested we were diplomats, and our belongings shouldn't be touched. "From what country, Russia?" scoffed the chief, in a voice so sarcastic that it worried me. Perhaps he hadn't been told.

"You can get twenty-five years to life for spying," the other customs' officer informed us. "We have notified the RCMP, and they are on their way." So far they hadn't searched me, and the film was burning a hole in my pocket. The scary thing was I knew I would hide the film even if it were the real thing and we were playing for higher stakes, in Russia or anywhere else.

We were told that Bill Jones had already been taken to Cornwall for processing. They were lying. After we protested our innocence for a few minutes more, we were taken to a room across the hall where the now very white-faced Prague-bound attaché and his grim-faced wife waited. "Sit down," our captors demanded, and I wondered what was going to happen next. Were we going to be interrogated together?

Suddenly a screen flickered to life on the wall, and there we were, our roles as enemy agents captured on video. The scenario was over. We were all friends now and could relax. The video showed us as we had hoped to appear—poised, confident, and unafraid. A dynamic duo indeed. Appearances counted in tight situations, didn't they? Unfortunately the other couple didn't attempt our Batman and Robin act (what normal couple in their forties would, come to think of it). They hadn't joined in the spirit of the harassment at all. Flustered and annoyed, they seemed to take it all so personally. The contrast was embarrassing for all of us. I thought, "just as well you are only going to Prague." After all it had only been a game.

But any smugness we felt was tempered with the knowledge that soon the challenge would be coming from Soviet border guards, and we really would be foreign spies. Still, I wasn't deterred from our future assignment; I was looking forward to it even more. The training just aroused my curiosity and imagination. Really, it was all about being adventurous—after writing about other people's derring-do for years, I was ready for my own piece of real-life action and a role in the Cold War spy game fitted the bill nicely.

Our intelligence handlers wished us good luck and said they looked forward to seeing our material. If Ottawa's portrayal of what it was going to be like in the Soviet Union was only half-accurate, I was ready for my diplomatic passport immediately.

As it turned out, we would experience one of the most exciting times in Russia's history and probably in our lives.

4

In-Country

We took a British Airways flight into Moscow in early July 1991. I was a spy at last, and in-country. It was still the Soviet Union, and we quickly got a taste of what the country had been like for the past seventy years—the state stores, the lineups, the lack of food products, the government press and television, the unlit streets. With little money and no choice of goods, Muscovites stared at foreigners' clothes, examined their shoes, and studied their hairstyles and accessories.

The three modes of public transport—besides the efficient Moscow metro system—buses, electric trolleybuses and trams (both attached to overhead wires, the former on wheels, the latter on rails) dominated the roads along with the noisy, fume-belching dark khaki GAZ vans, and light blue KamAZ trucks. (The trucks bore the old-fashioned wartime look I remembered with glee from my training flashcards.) The huge black ZIL and Chaika cars carrying Kremlin officials; the ubiquitous black, beige, white, and red Lada Zhiguli, Samara, and Niva cars; and Moskvich and Volga automobiles made up most of the other vehicles. Money difficulties for would-be car buyers, combined with all the red tape involved in the purchase, kept traffic numbers low. Ownership of a foreign-made car was a rarity.

By 2006 Muscovites' fashion chic has left us somewhat in awe and feeling like country cousins. The range of foodstuffs from around the world makes Canada's major supermarkets look rather provincial in comparison. Today's traffic-clogged Moscow streets, packed with Mercedes and BMWs, make the streets of 1991 an era long past.

But then Moscow was exactly as I had envisioned it and I savoured the untouched spookiness, whether real or imagined. Spying for me was a totally selfish endeavour, a thrilling experience. There was certainly no ideology involved. Russians probably didn't find it in the least bit romantic to live the reality, but I, in my excitement, couldn't believe my luck that the hostile environment for which I had trained was still intact. I'd seen the movies, read the books, and now was anxious to play the game.

Mind-boggling events were about to happen over the next few months. Perhaps, besides language, weaponry, and spying our training should have included some current Russian politics. The huge political struggle and infighting going on at the time pointed to some sort of final collapse. Gorbachev's glasnost had released a force that would destroy the Soviet Union. The speed with which the disintegration came about would take everyone by surprise, including the world's top political scientists and intelligence experts.

One only had to take a step into Sheremetyevo-2, Moscow's international airport, to experience the smell of the whole Soviet Union. Even today, a whiff brings back nostalgic memories. To me it wasn't really that unpleasant—dirty sour water mixed with body and food odour. Even the smells of spring in Paris or a summer evening in Hyde Park are mixed with diesel, fuel, and people perfumes as well as fresh rain, grass, leaves, and flowers. But this particular smell was everywhere, in shops, apartments, offices, and hotels. Renovations and new paintwork couldn't eliminate it. Perhaps today's snazzy new buildings will escape the smell for a while. But only if the cleaners learn to wash the floors and stairwells with lashings of cleaning products and not just push the same old recycled water about from floor to floor, stair to stair. The smell hovers in buildings in Russia and from Ukraine to Kazakhstan, Latvia to Georgia. I caught it on two Russians sitting next to me in a Second Cup café in Calgary and I once sat in a brand new Lada Niva in a dealership in Ottawa, just to get a recharge of that odour.

Sam, Katya (nineteen), James (sixteen), and I were given a temporary apartment as ours wasn't ready—it was still occupied by the couple we were there to replace. Katya and James were with us just for the summer holidays—Katya attended the University of Ottawa and James was a boarder at Trinity College School near Toronto. Charles, twenty-one, a student at Queen's University, was staying with his girlfriend, Miranda, in Calgary (they were to be married before our tour in Moscow ended).

The apartment had been empty for some time, and was overrun by very hungry cockroaches. It was located just a few blocks from the Russian parliament, referred to as the White House, and just a short walk from the building that housed our future permanent residence.

Our predecessor in the role of military attaché, Bob Weir, hung around long enough for a farewell dinner at the Aerostar, a Canadian-Russian joint venture hotel, where the foreign partner provides the money and management while the local side contributes the infrastructure and valuable people connections. Problems can occur when partners fall out and the Aerostar has suffered a few.

At the dinner we unfortunately had to witness Weir and his wife presenting the Russian chief of military liaison, Colonel General Mikhail Grivnov, with a red "Russian Express" credit card he'd had made up as a joke. The attaché thought it was humorous, the general did not. A credit card was just a dream for him then. But it was more prophetic than funny. Today, the retired general in Russia, a businessman, probably has a credit card with considerably more clout than that of a retired colonel in Canada.

The Weirs had yet another card to play before they moved from Moscow, although its nature was not revealed until a few months later: they supported their maid's departure to Canada and her subsequent defection. Although it was well known that most maids employed by foreigners reported to the KGB, I cannot imagine that their information was worth much. She either had some very clever story to tell or the Weirs just couldn't do without ironed underwear.

The military liaison office that General Grivnov ran was a branch of the GRU designated to look after foreign military attachés in the Soviet Union. Every country, including Canada, has a similar office for guiding the activities of foreign military attachés and answering their questions about military matters. Grivnov and his colleagues knew we were spies, because that's what western military attachés did in the Soviet Union in 1991. However, they had control over where we went and whom we spoke to because we had to seek their permission to travel and their approval for meetings. While our task was to use any means to unearth the latest information about equipment, troop strength, movements, activity at military-industrial complexes etc., the GRU's job was to foil our efforts. It did this by making its presence felt at every opportunity. Most of Grivnov's officers were ex-military attachés so they knew the routine. Violating the rules and being caught spying they knew meant expulsion—a diplomatic and political nightmare often resulting in tit-for-tat embassy oustings. Some had been kicked out of European countries, including the UK, during "usual suspects" military attaché roundups over the years. We saw a lot of them at diplomatic parties and receptions, and they were always humorous and friendly in a smooth and knowing sort of way that made me feel like the amateur spy I was.

Our new, permanent residence with its plush, beige, wall-to-wall carpet, was a large apartment by Russian standards then, with three bedrooms. It was decorated with fine furnishings and fabrics that had been brought in from Ottawa via the embassy. The drapes in the large living room were made of a dusty pink, silky material. Together with the sheers, they created the appropriate warm and inviting diplomatic look for guests. The windows looked down five storeys to the traffic and pedestrians on Bolshaya Dorogomilovskaya Street, about three blocks from the Moscow River and a main artery into the downtown core.

The kitchen had recently been renovated in a Scandinavian style—white and beech-coloured cupboards—with a new gas oven and dishwasher. The latter wasn't hooked up correctly, which I discovered only after a surge of electricity went through me as I touched the dishwasher door with one hand and the sink with another, but this was soon fixed by an electrician hired by the embassy. It was too early to blame this incident on KGB harassment. The repair probably saved our maid from possible death by electrocution, as the kitchen would be her domain. She came in every morning at nine.

The laundry room was also a storage room. Side-by-side with the European washer and North American dryer was the year's supply of dry food and household goods we had brought with us from Canada. This room was the favourite haunt of cockroaches. Wine, alcohol, and beer for entertaining were on open shelves in a small room off the main hall. After an incident with the commandant of the building, these shelves were later given doors. To most Soviets in 1991 we were living in unattainable comfort. Now, to many twenty-first-century Russians the apartment would seem very ordinary.

I had a letter of introduction from the Writers' Union of Canada to the Union of Soviet Writers and I acted on this as soon as we were all settled in our apartment in July. This was a personal thing to do with my being a writer, but still the intention had to be cleared with Ottawa. My overtures to the union would not go unnoticed by the Soviet secret police. Writer or not, a foreigner just couldn't turn up anywhere without a check being made, and I was the bearer of a special identity card issued by the Ministry of Foreign Affairs to diplomats of a certain ilk.

Ottawa didn't mind, thinking I might usefully glean insight into the "current mood" of the country's intelligentsia. My contact person was the well-known writer and film director, Vladimir Zheleznikov, who took me along to a union meeting. Prior to the business we ate caviar, cold meats, and smoked salmon and drank Russian champagne in the ornately carved, wood dining room of the union's mansion on Gertsena Street, where decades of Soviet writers had relaxed. Their photographs hung on the walls, including one of Vladimir's father-in-law, Konstantin Paustovski, a Nobel Prize nominee in 1965.

Although embarrassed by my Russian in such grammatically correct company, I learned my host was a household name throughout the Soviet Union for a children's book he had written called *Chuchelo* (Scarecrow). It had become a children's classic and then a popular movie. Vladimir introduced me to writers from all parts of the Soviet Union who had gathered in Moscow for the meeting and announced my presence from the podium. Neither this two-bit Canadian writer nor the cream of the craft from the far-flung states could envision that within a few months the famous union would cease to exist and its place would be taken by new writing organizations in fifteen different countries. Their ornate meeting place would eventually become an expensive private restaurant.

Afterwards Vladimir drove me back to my apartment building on the other side of the Moscow River. "Drop me here," I said well before my turnoff. For Vladimir's sake I didn't want the nosey KGB-employed guards in the compound to see who was driving the wife of the building's newest military attaché. Vladimir caught on and was bemused. To a sixty-something survivor of the Soviet Union, and a famous one to boot, I was slightly overrating my significance. Fortunately our friendship survived my naivety. It was my first step down the path of becoming Russified.

In late July, Katya and James stayed in Moscow while we took a trip to Leningrad (St. Petersburg) with the Canadian naval attaché, John Mason, and his wife, Diane. The Masons were on their second tour of duty in Moscow. Fresh from our training in Canada, it was our first chance to experience Soviet train travel, stay in a genuine Soviet hotel, and professionally explore our first large Soviet city. It was also our first opportunity to encounter the real KGB. Our excitement was drum level, but we hadn't yet adopted our spy demeanour, still midway between touristy enthusiasm and world-weary traveller. Hence the presence on the initial sorties of wiser, more experienced partners.

Mason was a tall, straightlaced, humourless navy type with a permanently worried look. He was very good about imparting, in a fatherly fashion, all of his acquired knowledge about Russia. His wife made up for his lack of charisma and humour and her Russian was better. She was warm, gregarious, and laughed easily. Although she overwhelmed some, I liked her. "Buy a car and get out and about on Moscow's roads," was her early and sound advice to me.

Long-distance train travel in Russia was quite comfortable, for diplomats anyway, who travelled in deluxe carriages. The compartments contained two bunk beds, which folded into padded bench seats during the day, and a fold-down table for picnics. The conductress in charge of our carriage provided a hot cup of tea from her electric samovar. It came in a glass held in a silver container decorated with the emblem of Soviet Union railways. We persuaded her to sell us two. Within months this kind of Soviet memorabilia would be on sale among the Lenin statues and military uniforms at various flea markets in Moscow.

The train stations were full of the usual seething humanity, cardboard suitcases, and Chinese plastic, checkered bags, but there was none of the fighting for tickets and vying for seats for us. The tickets had been purchased in advance and picked up by an embassy driver and we only had to wait on the platform to board. The embassy supplied a special metal bolt for the compartment door as extra security. There had recently been a rash of foreign travellers being gassed and robbed while they slept their way through the countryside. We did seem like easy targets, cocooned in our deluxe compartments under the rough but clean sheets, pillows, and blankets while ordinary Russians shared cluttered carriages of bunk beds or sat up all night. But like the robbers, the KGB, who also rode the rails, would not have had it any other way—they knew where to locate us. On our train two likely members of the security agency shared copious amounts of tea with the conductress. For that reason we never left our compartment unattended on our trips to the toilet or when stretching our legs in the corridor.

We stayed at the Astoria Hotel in Leningrad. Of the city's grander hotels, it was considered to be in the best condition; all needed refurbishing, and all have now been restored to their former glories. The Astoria's advantage is its historic setting in a square dominated by golden-domed St. Isaac's Cathedral and a monument to the Russian ruler Nicolas I. Its former atmosphere is only a haunting memory now that it has been handsomely reborn as part of Sir Rocco Forte's collection of luxury hotels.

A car from the state travel agency Intourist met us at the train station. Official taxis were few and far between then and the state frowned on diplomats hiring so-called "gypsy cabs"—any private passenger vehicle you could stop by standing on the side of the road and extending your arm. Although it was a sunny July morning there were no tourists milling around the square as we pulled up at the Astoria. Nevertheless, there were quite a few people, mainly men, swarming inside the front entrance as we pushed our way through to the reception desk.

Of course we were expected. Everyone on the desk would have been informed of our military status and knew that the new arrivals were spies. Although we tried to look relaxed and I felt a bit like I was on holiday, we did look more determined than touristy. We knew that the secret police would shadow us inside the hotel as well as on the streets and that mingling among the lobby crowd would be our minders getting a close look at us. We were also aware that all the staff of any international Soviet hotel was automatically an employee of the state and therefore reported to internal security.

But all foreigners were treated with suspicion, not just us. Visiting diplomats, businessmen, government officials, and tourists would all be under scrutiny. Mix these hotel guests with the local citizenry who could afford Astoria prices, or bribes to the doormen, including black marketeers, government cronies, and people with information to sell in exchange for dollars or immigration, and you had an atmosphere full of clandestine meetings and furtive activity.

Our large, airy room was furnished in a Soviet style with a dark wood and glass china cabinet containing enough dinnerware for a small party, a table and four chairs, two single beds, and red, crushed-velvet bedspreads and curtains. The ensuite bathroom was functional and the toilet was better than the one on the train.

The best thing about the Astoria was that it was within walking distance from all the city's cultural attractions. We fell in love with Leningrad. If we were followed, we didn't care; if someone was playing tricks on us, we were enjoying the delights of the Hermitage too much to notice. I had read about Kafe Literaturnoe in the city's historic heart and we managed to get a table. We ate red and black caviar on rounds of bread as a classical quartet and then a female opera singer entertained us. Perhaps those two men at the table next door were listening to our conversation. But so what? Maybe we could think of something to say that would make their night.

Our travelling companions were a reminder that we were on a three-day working trip not a vacation. We gaped at the stunning architecture of the buildings but also managed to note the large naval college housed in the old Admiralty on Dvortsovaya Ploshchad (Palace Square) and the army and police presence there.

And we spoke Russian at every opportunity. John and Diane stepped back to let us buy fruit at a local market, negotiate a train schedule change, hire a car from Intourist, order meals, and pay bills. The trip allowed us to feel more comfortable with the Russian environment—when we returned to Moscow it was like coming home.

In early August we visited Helsinki because we were also accredited as diplomats to Finland and had to present our credentials. Katya and James were getting used to being left in Moscow alone. It was a safe city before the fall of Communism—women and children could feel quite comfortable, day or night, travelling alone on the metro, hailing unofficial taxis, or walking the dimly lit streets. Besides, our building, which housed foreign journalists and diplomats, had a secure parking lot guarded by men working for the KGB, and the Canadian embassy was only a telephone call away. So when we made plans to be away in Latvia in mid-August, leaving them in the apartment, it gave us little concern.

We were to leave on the late-night train on August 18. We spent the day picnicking beside a small tributary of the Moscow River. It also happened to be beside Tushino, a military base just outside of Moscow, where an air show was being held. We had our cameras with us of course. At one point, the first public performance of a Soviet Union aerobatic team ever seen by Canadian military attachés flew over our heads in an exciting and colourful display. Used to watching dull films of single flying aircraft in a basement in Ottawa, we were awed by the swift, spectacular demonstration. We didn't know that it was our first and last glimpse of an air display team flying under the Soviet flag. The next time, at another air show at a military base in Zhukovsky near Moscow, it would be Russian.

August 19, 1991 was to be a fateful day for the Soviet Union.

5

Coup d'état

Since the second half of the 1980s, Mikhail Gorbachev's perestroika (reconstruction) reforms had unintentionally unleashed long-suppressed nationalistic feelings in the Soviet Union's republics and they had begun calling for greater independence from Moscow. The declining Soviet economy wasn't helping matters. To appease the fifteen states, Gorbachev had agreed to sign a new Union Treaty making them independent republics in a much looser federation with a common president. That treaty was due to be signed on August 20.

Blissfully unaware of any new political drama, we boarded the train for Latvia at midnight on August 18, following our day at Tushino. We were again with John and Diane Mason, whose first posting to Moscow had been in the eighties. But even with his experience, Mason had no way of knowing about the earth-shattering event that was to take place the next morning on August 19. Coup plotters were at work even as we boarded the train to the Baltic country—putting Gorbachev under house arrest at his holiday home on the Crimean coast. But in our compartment, this time with four bunks, we all slept closely but soundly.

We put the train radio on just before eight in the morning. Radio

Moscow's hourly news was beginning. The report was incredible. There was a new government in place. Had we heard correctly? To make sense of the broadcast, heavily laden with propaganda, we scrambled for our short-wave radio and the BBC. Gorbachev had been deposed, and there were tanks on the streets of Moscow.

News spread fast and worried passengers gathered in the corridors. Here we all were on a train hundreds of miles from the capital. Muscovites wished they had stayed in Russia while Latvians couldn't get home fast enough.

Arriving at our Intourist skyscraper hotel in the centre of Riga (now refurbished as one of Latvia's premier hotels) we immediately booked seats on the next train back. There were many people struggling for tickets, but we finally managed to get a compartment for late that night. Sam tried telephoning Katya and James from our room, but the hotel operator informed him that lines to Moscow were unavailable. The new political drama added a chill to her words, even though telephone connections in the Soviet Union were notoriously unreliable.

Hungry after our long train ride, we ate lunch in the hotel's twenty-sixth-floor restaurant that looked out on the old part of the city with its cobblestone streets and art nouveau buildings. Suddenly, someone shouted "tanks" and everyone left their tables to stare down at the column making its way through the streets of Riga.

We were witnessing a major historic and potentially tragic event: a coup in Moscow followed by Soviet tanks on Latvian streets. Our job was to report the happenings as best we could, and we took photographs and videotaped the army advancing from barracks within the city and outside. But we were aware of the people around us, who had experienced Soviet domination for decades, and who were displaying both despair and fear. What was going to happen next? We had to get to the streets to find out.

We had already arranged to meet with an Intourist representative to take us on a walking tour of the city at two o'clock and decided to stick with the plan despite the fact that when the guide arrived he was visibly nervous. "There are tanks on the streets. The radio station, post office, and telegraph office are surrounded by Soviet troops," he said. He clearly was hoping we were going to cancel the tour so that he could go home to his family. But we required a local guide even more urgently now to take us to all the hot spots as quickly as possible, and asked him to work with us as long as he could. "Then you can go home," we told him. He sighed but plunged with us onto the streets.

As we walked towards the city centre, fully armed Russian helicopters circled threateningly overhead. We photographed them and took pictures of scared shoppers in the main market stocking up on food. Mason videotaped the scene with his small camcorder. Our guide didn't want to go anywhere near Soviet troops, but we insisted on going to the communications building, which included the telegraph and post offices that they were already guarding. It had become a gathering point for Latvians and there was a rumbling of discontent mounting from the crowd. Nevertheless, they kept their distance from the soldiers, who held Kalashnikov assault rifles and were supported by armoured personnel carriers (APCs).

We clicked away and through the camera lens I saw the determined faces of the troops. They had been ordered onto the streets to quell any uprisings. Their orders came from Moscow hundreds of miles away. As it turned out they came from hapless plotters, unstable and vindictive leaders who had decided to stage a coup d'état while President Gorbachev was vacationing on the Black Sea, but these soldiers were dangerously oblivious to all that. Nor did they know that in Moscow the Russian parliament was counter-coup headquarters and barricades had been built to repel Soviet troops. Nor that some of their compatriots close to the parliament building, the White House, had already switched sides to Russian president Boris Yeltsin after he had stood astride one of their tanks and damned the coup and the attack by the Soviet army.

Even Latvian officials in the know would have held their breath. Gorbachev was still a prisoner in his summer home. Martial law had been declared in Russia. The Russian parliament was the linchpin. If it went and Yeltsin was ousted by Soviet troops, the Baltics would surely feel a backlash. In nearby Lithuania just the previous January 20, civilians had died in clashes with the Soviet Army after Lithuania had been so bold as to declare its independence from the Union.

Fortunately the coup was failing. It had been staged by diehard Communists in the party apparatus, the military, and the KGB, for whom the signing of the Union Treaty due to take place on August 20 was the last straw. Incompetence, poor planning, military discord, and the will of the people were against the plotters; their scheme was imploding. But it would be twenty-four hours before Latvians, under the threat of Kalashnikovs and helicopter gun ships, would feel relief, and then freedom.

The air was menacing and our Latvian guide had become an incoherent wreck. We let him go home and returned to the hotel to again try to contact Moscow. Sam reached the embassy but still couldn't connect with our children. He spoke to Sergeant Terry Meader, who said he would arrange for someone to check on our apartment. He added he was sure Katya and James were fine as one of the security guards had seen them at the embassy that morning borrowing videos. Borrowing videos while a coup raged? That seemed too cool for our comfort.

As evening approached Sam and I, along with the Masons, decided to go out into the city streets again. The helicopters were still in action but now people were becoming bolder and there were huge numbers everywhere. Perhaps they'd had news from Moscow about the people defending the Russian parliament and thought it could happen in Riga. The commander of the troops guarding their city was not so easily won over. He was following strict orders, not realizing that this coup was the start of a major revolution that would see him gone from Latvia within a few months and his troops with him. But that night he was in charge and we were Western spies prowling through his territory.

I don't know who first saw the armoured personnel carriers coming towards us. We were between them and the communications building and it was obvious that that's where they were heading. The APCs were firing above the crowd and the bullets flew over our heads. Every fifth round produced tracers which illuminated the scene. The latter looked like horizontal fireworks and I was fascinated by the deadly display. I remember thinking, "I've always wanted to see real tracer bullets."

Then I was roughly pulled down to the ground. Perhaps I was over-trained. Fearless. Everyone was on the ground now. The Masons were crouching behind a clump of trees, albeit very young trees. My husband and I crawled over to them. "Firefights are not spectator sports," John Mason reminded us sternly.

The APCs, with heavily armed troops aboard, continued firing as they roared and rattled by. Fortunately, we, and those around us, escaped being hit. Some Latvians standing in and around the telegraph and post office buildings were not so lucky that night.

In a subdued mood, we walked to the hotel. We moved quickly and quietly and didn't say a word in English. Patrolling soldiers were everywhere, army vehicles rattled by, and there was a column of tanks coming out of a barrack area near the hotel. If things were somewhat under control in Moscow, they were unpredictable in Riga.

We had to get our bags for the train and make more phone calls. I finally reached James, who said he and Katya had woken late. They'd walked to the Canadian embassy to borrow some videos "through all these tanks and soldiers and people near the White House." Apparently Katya, who besides being a student was a part-time model, had caught the Russian troops' attention. My son described how the tank turrets, their muzzles already adorned with flowers from optimistic Muscovites, had swivelled in her direction to enable the *tankists* to watch her as she did her runway walk down Kutuzovsky Prospekt and across Kalininsky Bridge. Since she is shortsighted she probably didn't notice.

Neither of them had a clue that they were witnessing a historic event. They thought it was just another armed forces day celebration. As they were leaving the embassy with an armful of videos the security guard had said, "Be careful out there." But they thought he was talking about the traffic. No one mentioned a coup. When they got home they switched on the television and caught the pictures on CNN. "Hey, that looks like Moscow." Now they were getting ready to go out again to see what was going on. "No, don't do that," I said, remembering the bullets. "Stay in the house. We'll be there tomorrow." That was the night three young Russians died in an underpass near the American embassy in a skirmish between enthusiastic White House defenders and nervous *tankists*. When we arrived back in Moscow early on August 21, people still milled about the burned-out buses and abandoned tanks that had been involved in the encounter. Already the men were heroes and a memorial of photographs and flowers had sprung up above the place where they had died.

Abandoned buses still blockaded the area near the White House. Ambassadors, foreign diplomats, and journalists were on the streets recording the events and trying to make sense of what was happening. The ears of the people around us were pressed to *Echo Moskvy*, a defiant little radio station that continued to broadcast real news of the coup while all other Russian media either ceased or broadcast only propaganda. Suddenly the cry went up from the crowd, "We've won. The *putsch* is over." But what the arrest of the coup plotters and the retreat of the army really meant for Soviets at that point would have been hard for anyone to imagine.

The elite tank corps that hours earlier had thundered menacingly down Kutuzovsky Street towards the Russian parliament was withdrawing. In our small Zhiguli car we followed their retreat, filming and taking pictures. The route took us to the Tushino military base, the very place where we had watched the brilliant Soviet air display just a few days before.

The huge army we saw assembled there amazed us. Had the coup succeeded, and the Soviet hierarchy been replaced by the schemers, that military strength might have been theirs and history would have been rewritten a very different way. The coup leaders included Vladimir Kryuchkov, chairman of the KGB, and Gorbachev's own vice-president, Gennady Yanayev; both the secret police and the army had supported the plotters when they had announced their initial "state of emergency." But that was before they realized how weak the coup really was.

When we were training in Canada and studying Soviet armament we had been told that we might catch a "glimpse" of new tanks, APCs, or heavy artillery, but here it was, the might of the Soviet Army, arrayed before us like an intelligence gatherer's dream. We sat in our car and watched, mesmerized, as tank by tank, truck by truck, the army rolled out onto the road in front of us, heading for Moscow's Outer Ring Road. We had enough footage to keep Ottawa going for months. We even joined the convoy in formation and shot video and film. It went on forever and we gave up counting as we drove back and forth. No one bothered to stop us although it was apparent who we were. We had red diplomatic plates and, to top it off, Sam's licence number was "007." We didn't know it then, but the fact that everything was so openly on display to us was a sign of things to come.

We got back in time for a dinner party at the home of the British air attaché, the date, August 21, having been arranged weeks before. Dinner parties were more than just social events, they were business meetings, albeit pleasant ones with good food and drink. Coming so soon on the heels of the coup this one was particularly animated. All gatherings like ours were spied upon through the various methods used by the GRU or KGB, but that night the listeners were virtually ignored.

Already some republics, including Latvia, had taken the opportunity to declare their independence. Although a curfew was still in place in Moscow, only the maids left early. Who called the curfew and when? In the circumstances it was difficult to know. And besides, our diplomatic immunity normally covered such government bans. The attachés, mostly from western embassies, had been out and about like us, though none had been to the Baltics, and we compared notes on the three days. Most thought that the outcome of the events, the stand by Yeltsin, and the way the army had wavered and retreated, boded well for the future. In those days, friendly contact with members of the Soviet military was rare. None of us envisioned that the changes to come would include animated Russian military leaders and their wives joining us at our homes for drinks and dinner parties.

All our gathered material was sent to Ottawa by diplomatic bag or encrypted e-mail. On August 22, Diane Mason and I walked Moscow's streets, watching for any sign of military or secret police activity, and scanning newspapers and listening to the radio and television. Sam was involved with meetings at the embassy with the ambassador Michael Bell. Bell had also returned on the third day of the coup. He had been on a bicycling holiday in Holland with his family. Stopping to ask someone for directions he had been told about the Soviet *putsch*. He almost fell off his bicycle and was on the next plane back to Moscow.

During the evening, we welcomed the new Swiss military attaché at a reception at his embassy. Again we compared notes and exchanged new information. Events were unfolding quickly. Yeltsin was not going to give up the momentum gained by his actions during the coup and it was a weakened Gorbachev who now faced the Soviet people. Before he even returned to Moscow from the Crimea, his political rival Yeltsin had already signed a decree banning the Communist party throughout Russia. This ban was soon extended throughout the Soviet Union and seventy years of Communist rule came to an end. Gorbachev was further humiliated by Yeltsin by being forced to read publicly the doctrine of the coup plotters, all former Soviet ministers. They were now awaiting trial, save one, a military general who had committed suicide. Despite Gorbachev's efforts, the Soviet Union was unravelling.

We were out again on Friday night, August 23, at the home of the Canadian embassy's minister-counsellor for commercial and economic affairs, Richard Mann. This kind of social calendar wasn't unusual for military attachés in Moscow but now meeting together had become much more important. That night the discussion focused on just one issue: what is next for the Soviet Union? We talked for hours but were still not satisfied with our conclusions. When it was almost time to go home, I was looking at the city from the apartment high above Oktyabrysky Square (named after the 1905 October Revolution) when someone suggested we should take a drive around Moscow. We were missing history while talking about it. What was going on out there? How were the Soviet people reacting?

En masse we roared away in our little Zhigulis and headed for KGB headquarters, the backbone of the Soviet Union and location of the infamous underground prison, Lyubyanka. Our instincts were right: the square in front of the building was alive with people.

If ever there was confirmation that the Soviet Union had changed forever in the space of five days it was the view of hundreds of Muscovites feverishly and noisily pulling down the statue of Dzezhinsky, the founder of the dreaded secret police, right under the nose of the KGB. The statue was down, lying across the grassy embankment that had surrounded it. The crowd cheered. There was no interference from any officials at all. Besides, hadn't Yeltsin defied the very people Dzezhinsky represented? The genie was coming out of the bottle and the KGB had more important things to worry about—like its masses of incriminating Soviet files and the future of its members.

All that remained of the statue was the marble base with its inscription. Determined to do our bit to help knock Dzezhinsky into oblivion we joined the crowd. One member of our party had a tire iron in the trunk of his car and after a few swift blows we all had our own pieces of marble, souvenirs of the night. I did have a few qualms about whether diplomats should be destroying historical monuments, and what Ottawa would think about it, but the jubilation of the Russian dismantlers was infectious and there were certainly no KGB agents around to record our indiscretion.

Of course a monstrous organization like the KGB (now called the Federal Security Service) would survive the fall of Communism, even though many of its agents defected with documents containing succulent secret tidbits, others went into private business, and the agency was "nationalized" by each of the fifteen former Soviet states. It was the smaller law enforcement agencies that would be demoralized and destroyed. Corruption, low wages, and the lack of willpower in local police precincts have now led to some overwhelming and unsolvable criminal activity in Russia.

No one had predicted the momentous events of August 1991, not even the most ego-driven of historians who called themselves Sovietologists. They were racing to catch up. As the Soviet Union began to fly by the seat of its pants we wondered how it would affect our situation.

6

"Friends"

When Katya and James left to go back to university and boarding school respectively, it was early September. The crumbling Soviet Union hadn't yet completely dissolved into fifteen independent states, but the pace of change was unstoppable and by year's end the USSR had effectively disintegrated. As each new state emerged, countries worldwide embraced them.

Nevertheless, there were no new orders from Ottawa to change our direction and spying was still the order of the day, with special emphasis on what the military was up to. The latter, with millions of members from hundreds of different ethnic backgrounds in the Soviet Union, was staying remarkably quiet amid the turmoil. And quiet wasn't always a good thing according to long-time Cold War observers.

So, now well rehearsed, Sam and I took an Aeroflot plane ride to Novosibirsk in Western Siberia. It was our first face-to-face encounter with on-the-job KGB agents. It was also our first serious spying operation.

We flew by the Russian workhorse, the Tu-154. Some foreigners are frightened to fly in this aircraft. One Canadian ambassador in Central Asia was so scared that he took the train everywhere, regardless of how long it took. The Tu-154 is old and has had its share of crashes. But fifteen years later it is still flying commercially. The plane itself is sturdy in the rough Soviet way. Russian pilots are professional and as good as any in the world. The worry is the maintenance and the lack of spare parts.

The meal on the four-hour flight was a strong cup of tea from a huge enamel kettle, a pale and cold boiled chicken leg, and a biscuit. Despite the unattractiveness of the food, we ate it hungrily.

Apart from the fact that "everyone" knew we were there (we had to get permission for trips from the Russian military liaison office and the foreign ministry), we seemed to be the only Westerners in town so stood out like raw recruits in our Canadian Mountain Equipment Co-op jackets, with our black leather camera bags and small knapsacks Our main mission was to observe and photograph a Russian air base on the outskirts of town. Was it business as usual? How many aircraft were there? Were they flying? Was there anything new with respect to the sounds of planes, shapes of hangars? The usual attaché questions, but more urgent because of the August events. While secret satellite imagery and communication interceptions are important spy tools, the horizontal view provided by human spies is still necessary; consider the flawed intelligence used to justify the Iraq war.

But that operation was going to be on the second day of our visit. We had the first day to ourselves. We grabbed a few hours' sleep after our night flight from Moscow.

The Intourist hotel was considered to be one of the best of its time; it had recently been built by a Turkish company. The suite had a bedroom with two single beds and a living area. We locked the door and Sam placed a chair under the handle. He said he had a feeling about the place. He was right. We were awakened after about an hour when the chair fell to the ground with a crash as someone pushed open the door. My husband leapt out of bed and looked out into the corridor. There was only a woman on her hands and knees a few yards away, polishing the floor furiously. She did not look up.

Before we left the room to explore the city, the telephone rang. It was hung up without a word when Sam answered. The KGB was just making sure they hadn't missed us. It was common practice for military attachés to do a tour of the city shortly after arriving at the hotel and the secret police were hinting we should begin.

The Soviet Union built cities that were easy to get around and thus to spy in. It was just as well, given the scarcity of maps. The old Soviet saying was: "If you need a map you are probably in a place where you shouldn't be." The maps that were available were wrong or had big blank spaces where the "interesting" buildings were located. But once you knew the downtown of one Soviet city in the provinces and republics, you knew them all. The government offices were built around a square where military parades and people's holidays could be celebrated. The huge statue on the square was usually Lenin. KGB headquarters were close by as were one or two Intourist hotels. Then there was the post office and telegraph building, the radio, television, and communications tower, a *militsia* (police) building, and a few military barracks. All were located on wide, tree-lined streets with an intricate array of overhead trolley-bus and tram wires. From east to west, north to south, the omnipresent concrete apartment blocks of the Soviet era made up the rest of the picture.

One whirl around the city and a spy knew where to find buildings of interest. It was the added attractions that made many cities of the former Soviet Union worth a return trip: Baku with its frontage on the Caspian Sea; Almaty and its Tien Shen Mountains separating it from China; Odessa on the Black Sea; Erevan in range of Mount Ararat; historic Kiev in Ukraine; and the artists of Krasnodar, to mention a few. If you like to tour all sorts of interesting places at no cost (except to the taxpayer), spy for your country. I think there are always vacancies.

An Intourist tour of the city would give us our first look at Novosibirsk. We booked it at the desk and waited for our guide. She was a pleasant Russian woman in her thirties and spoke reasonable English. With state-run Intourist the KGB knew we were in safe hands and could relax. The guide would tell us what we wanted to know. She would tell them what we wanted to know. It was a "we-know, they-know" situation and one we recognized from our training in Canada. I had to keep reminding myself that in Novosibirsk it was the real thing.

The guide was obviously proud of her city and we liked the look of it too. One of the biggest cities in the Soviet Union, Siberia's capital city boasted the usual state art gallery, museum, and opera and ballet theatre (one of the largest in Russia, according to our guide) but it was its clean, wide streets that impressed us. Not much traffic then, which added to the stark look. She pointed out the huge central railway station that had been architecturally designed like an imperial palace in 1939 and the reconstruction work taking place on the Alexander Nevsky Cathedral.

We didn't tax her with questions, such as how the Moscow coup had affected Siberians. She thanked us by asking the driver of the Niva four-by-four to stop and let us take some scenic photographs. We were on the other side of the stately Ob River, away from the downtown.

We jumped out of the vehicle to take a look. Perhaps a view of the city from here would be nice. Then we noticed what the background would be—both the old and new bridges that spanned the river and linked one part of Novosibirsk with the other. Unfortunately, bridges were considered strategic locations and taking pictures of them was not allowed by the authorities; not with KGB sympathizers present anyway. We turned the other way and saw smokestacks of industrial plants and in the distance a couple of antennae. Even worse. "I'll take a photograph of you," said the guide when she noticed our hesitation; it was part of her business to try to take an "entrapment" picture. We declined. Bridges and factories are not nice subjects to have on a film that might fall into the hands of the KGB. It could be used against us sometime in the future. We drove back to the city and left our guide, thwarted, at the hotel. We then set off again, this time on foot.

We scanned the shops. Using Moscow as a yardstick we wanted to see if there was more or less food, drugs, clothing, liquor, and household items available. Soft spying, I suppose, but someone somewhere made sense of the social scenes we sent them. The standard of living seemed much the same. As usual the children were nicely dressed, the girls with bows in their plaited hair, the boys in clean shirts with short-cropped hair. Russian parents, a lot of them single mothers, sacrificed and worked hard for their offspring.

As we walked, my eye caught sight of a store selling fur hats and we stopped suddenly. Everyone on the street around us stopped at the same time. Then our minders neatly recovered and looked in shop windows, read newspapers, stood at bus stops, and continued driving. But they had been caught out, and quite by accident. We went inside the shop and tried on a few hats but didn't buy any.

Back outside, the street started up again. We hoped they wouldn't be as aggressive as our trainers had been in Canada when we accidentally caused them to give their presence (called "burning") away. We had our own map of the city's strategic locations hidden in an inside pocket of my husband's jacket. It had been devised from earlier attaché visits to the city and was drawn up on rice paper. But we didn't dare consult it. After our guided tour, we had a good idea of where the sites were located and walked leisurely past the buildings housing the KGB, the police, the regional government, and military headquarters without having any interference from our escorts having to consult the map, or eat it. We were looking for any changes to state infrastructure or personnel. Were barracks bursting with troops? Did transportation look broken-down? Were communications between the military, KGB, and police working? (It was easy to confirm the latter.) Small pieces of information that helped Ottawa piece together what was happening in the regions.

That evening there was a cabaret in the hotel restaurant and after dinner we drank some Georgian wine and watched the entertainment. We enjoyed the local singers and musicians and even joined others on the dance floor, though we still clutched our small knapsacks—weird foreigners. It was very pleasant and no one bothered us, although we were supposedly in enemy territory, and tomorrow people would try to outwit us as we tried to collect material and information to send back to our government. I wondered how Soviet spies felt in countries like Canada the night before a mission. The same as us, I suspected, if they were military attachés. It was a job, an exciting one with a dash of personal danger—a clash of wits in an exotic location and under unusual circumstances. But there was no guilt. I reasoned that in my case it was because I'd spent so many years separating my real self from stories and issues as an author and journalist. This job was creative too and the experience somewhat similar: the same feeling of excitement as the information was collected and the project unfolded and the same enjoyable sense of accomplishment when it was over. This was the best "story" I had ever been on. Perhaps really good spies had a more serious approach.

The next morning there was an early-morning call from our silent KGB friends, which subdued us a little before we set off for the Russian air base. But once we hit the wide city sidewalks it became once more a game.

We weren't easy spies to follow. Not because we were clever and deceitful, but because we were indecisive. Is this the correct bus or not? Should we be on this trolleybus? Shall we stay on this tram or get that one? There's something interesting in that shop window, let's get off and take a look ... This can play havoc with followers.

We had the numbers of the public transportation we were supposed to take to an airforce base carefully written down on another piece of rice paper; once again, the information had come from files in the military attachés' office in Moscow's Canadian embassy. Buses, trolleybuses, and trams—all three have their special tickets and assigned stops. I had once innocently got on a bus in Moscow with a trolleybus ticket and was ordered to pay 30,000 roubles by a dubious-looking inspector for wrongful passage. Aided by horrified passengers, mainly babushkas, who berated the man that the real fine was about 300 times less than that, I managed to slip off the bus and melt away.

We found the right stop for the bus (marked A for *avtobus*) and got on a number seven. Knowing where to transfer to a trolleybus was tricky. But we suddenly saw we were approaching a main street with electric overhead trolleybus wires and jumped off. At least half the passengers descended the stairs with us. We knew we had to go north on the trolleybus and then catch a tram west. But nobody was going anywhere in a hurry—there was a power outage and all the trolleys were stopped in a line along the road. A dozen people lounged about by the T for trolleybus (*troleybus*) sign post.

Then the trolleys all started to make their peculiar electrical humming sound and we boarded the rear of the first one to come along and stood in the back. We had punched our tickets, bought from a street kiosk, in the small machine provided before we realized we were on the wrong bus—it had turned sharply left and was going downhill! The vehicle was packed. Finally the doors opened with a clunk at the next stop and we got off, heading back up the hill. Four men and a woman had also made the same mistake, it appeared.

We walked to the nearest T stop. The next trolleybus came within five minutes. This time we got on at the front and sat down. Two men sat behind us. The other three boarded the rear.

At last we saw a street with tramlines. We left the trolleybus, and seven of us crossed the road. Then we realized we were going south not north, so we crossed back. Three men crossed back behind us. The tram came in two sections. We got on the first but it was already crowded. At the next stop we decided to go to the second section where there were fewer passengers. We jumped off hurriedly and ran back to the rear. The tram was already beginning to move. "Sorry," we said as we bumped into two men standing by the door. I knew by the hairs on the back of my neck that we were now standing with KGB minders.

Our stop was the last one on the line. We followed our directions up a grassy embankment and into a village of colourful wooden houses (*izbas*). The two men from the tram strolled about ten yards behind us chatting to each other in Russian. Our route took us through the village up to a high concrete wall surrounding the perimeter of the air base, commonly known to visiting foreign military as an attaché wall: these walls were not usually in good repair. They afforded good views through cracks in the concrete and had large spaces near the ground big enough for a person my size to crawl under and footholds in the crumbling concrete that would allow people to take photographs over the top.

With minders so close on our tail, though, we realized we couldn't go nearer to the fence. We didn't want to cut short our time in the Soviet Union by attempting silly, antagonizing behaviour. We would have to stay on the road that ran alongside the base and hope for something to take off over our heads. But it was a nice day for a walk and we continued looking at the one-storey houses. It was fall and the leaves contrasted picturesquely with the blue, green, and yellow homes. There was some construction work going on and we could see that they were putting in running water. This must have been cause for celebration for the residents. At the moment there were hand pumps located every second block. In an average Siberian winter it would have been very cold pumping water for everyday use. When we heard a plane taking off, we got out a camera and began taking photographs of the houses, also hoping to capture something flying overhead. As we paused, the men behind us stopped. They smoked a cigarette or two and then continued when we started walking again. It seemed all part of a familiar routine for them and they didn't seem to be watching us terribly intently.

We reached the end of the village and had to go back down to where the T sign for tram (*tramvai*) hung over the road. It seemed like an unsuccessful trip with more comedy than spy craft, but we reassured ourselves that the amount of activity by the KGB to prevent us from looking at the air base would tell Ottawa that, despite the near end of the Soviet Union, the military was still anxious to hide something from prying eyes. We had to be satisfied with that. Personally, I would have loved to have been able to snap a photograph of a new low-flying fighter. "Taken by the wife of an attaché," it would read as it was passed between trainee spies in the secret basement in Ottawa.

We didn't see our friends again that day. We knew that our outing had informed the KGB that it was business as usual for western spies. Nevertheless, on the plane back to Moscow the next morning the two agents who had followed us so closely around the village were sitting in the row ahead of us. One of them adjusted his seat so that the back came down almost in Sam's lap. "Mustn't do that to diplomats," he grunted in Russian, turning round and grinning at me as he moved his seat forward. They were being more bold and overt than was normal. Was it because they had been jolted by the happenings of the past month? The future didn't look bright for Soviet state employees. Dare they dream about a better life in a country such as Canada?

7

Cotton Country

We flew to Tashkent, the capital of Uzbekistan, in an Ilyushin 86, the huge Russian jumbo aircraft, in October 1991. Uzbeks always enjoyed close industrial ties with Moscow—their factories built the Ilyushin aircraft—and because of this important contribution they felt, and still do feel, a cut above the rest of Central Asia. They must find the huge discoveries of oil in Kazakhstan and the new wealth there particularly galling.

Tashkent was the fourth largest city in the Soviet Union after Moscow, Leningrad, and Kiev. It's an ancient city—dating back over 2,000 years—and was an important caravan crossroads on the Silk Road. Unfortunately, many of its historical buildings were lost in a major earthquake in the sixties, and it was rebuilt Soviet style, with the usual plethora of cheerless apartment blocks and monotonous government buildings. Fortunately, the city planners also included wide, leafy boulevards, parks with fountains, and large squares for celebrations.

It was the huge Ilyushin factory that was always central to the interests of visiting attachés. To view the factory, we had to catch a tram past the factory and then another tram to a cemetery that was adjacent to the huge hangars. The idea was the same as in

Novosibirsk, to look over the wall of the cemetery at the assembled aircraft or at least take photographs of one flying overhead. I hoped we'd be more successful with this activity report.

On the first tram going past the factory, we were staring intently at the building and looking at the workers going in the iron gates when an elderly babushka sitting opposite asked, looking at my watch, "*Skoljka*?" I was still intent on the factory and mistook her Russian for "How much is your watch?" instead of "What's the time?" Both can start with "*skoljka.*" I turned to her and said: "I'm sorry, much too expensive for you." The woman caught on to my misunderstanding and cackled loudly, showing only a brown tooth here and there. I felt foolish.

The factory had disappeared so we were off this vehicle and hopefully on to another to the cemetery. Two double trams were arriving. Which should we get on? Was it number three or four? We couldn't look at our tiny pencil-drawn map. The tramlines forked just a little way ahead. We jumped on number three. Several people jumped on after us. Then we decided no, we'd take a chance on the number four. Four people jumped off after us and as we jumped onto the first car of the next tram, two other people rushed to its rear. We asked the driver if he was going to the cemetery. No, wrong one. He let us off at a stop in time for us to board the other oncoming tram, and it headed out into the country with just a few people on board. Had we lost our local contingent of KGB?

No, they were all at the cemetery waiting for us. The three men lounging around the two gates did not look like normal, mid-week visitors to the dead. They were talking together and glancing our way. Two were dark haired, middle aged, one in a dull black leather jacket and the other a heavy woollen sweater and track pants. The third was fair haired, in his twenties, and wearing a jean jacket. Only one of the men looked Uzbek, the others were ethnic Russians. We walked away from them up the road until we were out of sight. Sam lifted me up to peer over the high wall into the vast, overgrown, eerily quiet cemetery. It looked like the sort of place in which one could be cornered behind a gravestone and done in. Never to be seen again.

But bravely we walked casually back and entered the cemetery. We walked among the graves for a while, reading the inscriptions, as if that was all we were interested in. What we wanted to do was get a look over the wall on the factory side of the cemetery. But always behind us we could hear the intrepid "pad-pad" of followers. There were no normal visitors or mourners placing flowers: just the Uzbek and one of the Russians up ahead leaning against a gravestone watching our approach. We took a sharp left down through the tangled grass back to the gate.

A tram was approaching and, feeling disappointed about the failed trip, we got on. Instead of changing trams though, we decided to get off and walk past the airplane factory this time, not ride. I had the bright idea of sneaking around some private garages—corrugated iron shelters with doors and padlocks—just before the factory grounds began. I thought I might be able to get another angle on the building and maybe some photographs.

I don't know who was more startled. This had obviously been chosen as a rest area for the KGB following us: as I walked up they fled into open garages and hid behind sheds. We continued up the road and past the factory gates. We looked in and about six or seven people looked out. They had been waiting for us. All in all, without doing much, we had managed to burn quite a lot of the opposition.

That evening we decided to go to the opera. It was warm, even though it had been raining, and we opted to walk. It wasn't long before we were aware of two figures behind us in the dark. They followed us all the way to the theatre. We were a bit late and they were strict about letting people in once the concert had started. But apparently the balcony had empty seats so they sold us tickets and we walked up the sweep of stairs towards the entrance doors. As we reached the gallery level we looked down and saw two men enter the foyer. They went over to the cashier and spoke to her. I didn't see them buy any tickets but they came over to the stairs.

The female usher on duty, not happy that we were late, pushed open the door reluctantly and showed us to our seats. As far as I could see we were the only ones in the balcony. She showed us to the front overlooking the stage and dress circle. It was dark. From that height, one needed binoculars to see the opera, which was about a local historical hero, sung in Uzbek. The door opened again, light entered, and feet walked down the slanting floor and stopped a row behind us. We were separated from the floor below by just a metal bar and behind us were two men, breathing heavily, presumably the two who had just followed us from our hotel. Had our boldness earlier in the day annoyed their KGB colleagues and therefore them? Perhaps we shouldn't have entered the cemetery when we saw so many of them. And then walking by the factory instead of going by tram? They wanted to spook us and, because we were a bit paranoid, they succeeded. I don't like balcony heights anyway and, given the close company, I couldn't pay attention to the plot unfolding on stage. After twenty minutes, Sam whispered, "Do you want to leave." I nodded. We hurried out down the stairs followed by the sounds of disapproval from the usher, and walked back to our hotel.

The next day we took a car tour of Tashkent and the surrounding cotton fields. Uzbekistan had provided the Soviet Union with its cotton, but since the country had declared its independence on September 1, nobody knew what was going to happen to the industry.

The growing of cotton had provoked a huge environmental disaster in Uzbekistan and neighbouring Kazakhstan with the shrinking of the Aral Sea. This catastrophe was caused by zealous Soviet planners who had deliberately diverted the water of the Syr-Darya and the Amu-Darya, the two rivers that fed the Aral Sea, to irrigate the vast cotton and agriculture fields of Kazakhstan, Uzbekistan, and

Turkmenistan. Up until the early sixties, the Aral Sea was the world's fourth-largest inland sea. But by the time we were in Uzbekistan it had already shrunk by half. As the sea diminished, it left towns and villages, once vibrant ports and fishing harbours, in desertlike conditions stranded many kilometres from the water. Adding to the calamity were the health problems caused by the contamination of rivers and drinking water by the pesticides, defoliants, and fertilizers used in cotton production.

Our Intourist guide, perhaps feeling she could talk more freely now that Uzbekistan had declared its independence, said that in the eighties many women became sick after working in cotton fields freshly sprayed with a toxic defoliant (similar to Agent Orange). Subsequently, many of these women's babies had died or suffered deformities at birth.

We could see workers in the fields, so reported that life in the countryside seemed much as usual. But soon the Soviet Union, the giant market for their cotton, would be no more. Being independent meant scrambling for new markets in a competitive economy. It would be a struggle that would last for years and is still ongoing. Not only was agriculture affected, but also industry, education, government, and the whole social infrastructure. The workers at the giant Ilyushin factory would be especially hard hit in the early days of independence as demand for the aircraft dropped.

8

Stomaching the Facts

Life was pleasant but busy in our Bolshaya Dorogomilovskaya Street home in the southwest of the city about three blocks from the Moscow River. Charles, Katya, and James had come home from school in Canada to spend Christmas 1991 with us and, along with other western military attachés and their families, we joined hundreds of celebrating Muscovites in Red Square on New Year's Eve. At the stroke of midnight we linked arms with our colleagues and other revellers and sang "Auld Lang Syne."

We were drowned out by a mighty display of fireworks and cheering as the red hammer and sickle flag of the Soviet Union was lowered beneath the Kremlin wall and the Russian flag with its three horizontal bands of white, blue, and red was hoisted, fluttering into the cold night. It was minus twenty degrees Celsius and the Russian champagne we'd brought along was quickly freezing to the edge of our glasses. Corks were popping all over the square as the noisy crowd of mostly young people drank to a new year and a new era—more than seventy years of Communist rule had officially ended.

Spying is closely connected with eating and drinking so we entertained and were entertained a lot, gleaning information at receptions, dinner parties, and over buffet meals. The Canadian government provided a budget for entertaining. This usually worked out to a formal dinner for twelve people twice a month or a buffet evening for twenty-four to thirty people once a month. Then there were the return dinner parties we attended and special functions at foreign embassies.

KGB or not, my maid and her helpers were all well trained by Canadian wives over the years in the niceties of entertaining and could turn out a dinner and dessert that the guests always praised. I provided the western meat—the most expensive part of the meal—and dairy products, purchased at foreign-run American dollar stores, and vegetables, fruits, salads, and flowers were obtained by the maids at the local markets with roubles I gave them. Most of the contents for sauces and desserts I kept in storage from Canada. Alcohol and wine were ordered through the embassy from a catalogue service in Stockholm.

The fillets of beef we began to buy from McDonald's (of hamburger fame). Opened near Pushkin Square in January 1990 by McDonald's Restaurants of Canada, the Moscow restaurant is the largest McDonald's in the world—it serves more than 30,000 people a day. The company developed its own farming and food-processing operations in Russia and sold its best meat, such as tenderloins, to foreigners and embassies. We could also buy their uncooked patties by the dozen and their own brand of buns. Now there are more than a hundred and twenty-five McDonald's in Russia in dozens of cities and more are planned.

Some attaché wives liked to impart their own touches to the dinners and shared cooking chores with the maids but I couldn't see the point. From the flowers decorating the table to the fine food, I couldn't see where I could do better. Guests always arrived at eight for pre-dinner drinks, except Russians who inevitably arrived early. I was sometimes surprised, always pleasantly, by what came out of the kitchen, and had to stop myself from saying, "Isn't this nice?" at the table.

Basil, our large Canadian cat, was always shut into a spare room until around ten. By then he was thoroughly wound up. Out he'd come and immediately mingle among the female guests, purring and begging for attention. It was a useful tool for entertaining foreign wives who didn't completely understand the language of conversation.

We'd found Basil in a humane society in Ottawa. Sam chose him because he resembled a wild cat complete with little tufts of fur on his ears. He enjoyed Moscow immensely because the maids brushed him every day and he no longer suffered fur balls. One maid even collected his fur and made it into a hat and mitts. Basil did not like his first encounter with the hat and pawed at it desperately when it was placed on a bed.

It happened that Gorbachev and his wife, Raisa, had a cat that was very similar to Basil. I cut out and framed a photograph from *Hello* magazine of the former president cuddling his cat. I didn't mind that visitors thought it was Basil.

The twelve people around the table nearly always included foreign diplomats and Russians. The Russians were mostly military generals (army, air force, or navy), their wives, and an accompanying "interpreter" from the military liaison office, sent to keep their top officers on the straight and narrow, and make sure they wouldn't be compromised and didn't get too drunk. After all, the friendly relationship between East and West was still very new.

During the early days the Russian generals were older, with grey hair brushed in the old-fashioned Brezhnev style, and very careful about what they said. But within a short while they'd mostly been replaced with younger, more debonair types—pilots and tank commanders who had a sense of humour. I found the navy captains usually remained more serious. Probably because their ships and submarines were still being shadowed aggressively on the high seas by us friendly, smiling foreigners. We were also still spying on their planes, but it was hard to remain really aggressive when later on

Russian test pilots started to offer Sam rides in their MiG-29 and MiG-31 fighter aircraft.

My favourite dinner guest was the chief of staff of the Russian air force, Colonel General Nikolai Denisov. He was disarmingly intelligent and funny. At all our dinners parties I got to entertain the two most important male guests at one end of the table (seating protocol putting them on either side of me), while my husband hosted their wives at the other. I was able to listen to and participate in some really good business conversation. I could also ask political questions with a smile and a laugh and get some good answers. The three remaining couples were arranged in appropriate male and female order in-between.

Arranging the seating around the table should have been a headache but it wasn't. Senior visitors, ambassadors, and generals, Russian ones over Westerners, were the priority guests and everyone else was happy to be fitted around them. After all, the food was just as good in the middle of the table, and one could still hear the conversation. And in the end, everyone got to be chief guest at someone's dinner at some time.

Official visitors were always arriving from Canada and one of our tasks was to escort them and generally look after them. Not long after our arrival, the Canadian army's top general arrived with one or two colonels. None of them had visited the former Soviet Union before. The Canadian general, Harry Wells, was relaxed in a rough, gruff army way and this went down well with his Soviet counterparts. He could also match his Russian hosts toast for toast and still remain upright. We held a buffet party at our apartment for everyone and the Canadian and Soviet generals sang duets of songs by Louis Armstrong and Frank Sinatra.

Because Wells and his Canadian party were being hosted by the Soviet army, they stayed at a hotel for senior military officers. One evening they enjoyed a visit to the famous Moscow Circus, but they didn't have time for supper beforehand. Sandwiches would be left in their rooms, they were told. It was after ten o'clock when they returned and flicked on the lights. What seemed like a black cover on the bread suddenly streamed off onto the floor and disappeared into the far corners of the room. A moveable feast of cockroaches.

Cockroaches were a constant problem. Although we had a maid who cleaned every day, one or two always appeared somewhere. As our dinner guests gathered in the living room for post-dinner coffee one night, I noticed that Basil was fixated on a cockroach rushing round and round inside a ceiling light fixture. Nothing would take the cat's mind off the sight until everyone was looking up.

We became used to the varieties—brown, black, small, large, flying—but our immediate reaction to seeing their fluttering antennae was always the same—kill! At a reception in the French embassy, a large cockroach stalked casually by the guests looking for crumbs on the floor. I stomped on it and then wished I hadn't—cockroach eggs are transported on soles of shoes. I rubbed my shoes vigorously on a rug before leaving the embassy.

Diane Mason had more than an insect problem; she had rats. She managed to slam the door on a retreating vermin but caught half his tail. The resulting squealing noise was terrible until she worked up the courage to open the door and free the mangled appendage.

Getting out of the apartment and meeting someone "for a coffee" took planning in Moscow then. I mean sitting down to a good cup of cappuccino in nice surroundings and just getting away from it all. One could buy a cappuccino at McDonald's even in those early days, but my favourite place was the Confectionery Café at the Hotel Metropol opposite the Bolshoi Theatre and not far from Red Square. I became very well known at the Metropol, since I also had my hair cut there, and the café would produce my cappuccino *nekrepki* (not strong) a few seconds after I arrived. It was an oasis away from thousands of moving bodies, cold weather, sidewalk sellers, vehicle pollution, Russian cigarette smoke, the steady hum of the metro's escalators, and the clang of the trolleybuses. Prices were the same as one would pay for a coffee in a five-star hotel in New York or Toronto, which meant the clientele then was exclusively foreign. But the frothy beverage was well worth it and I needed the break. The café had its own entrance from the street so customers didn't have to pass by the hard-eyed security guards in the hotel foyer. And it had nice toilets, important when one was in the centre of the city.

The hotel was unique because it was restored just prior to the fall of the Soviet Union. In 1985, Russian, German, Finnish, and Italian craftsmen and artists were hired to reconstruct the hotel to its original art nouveau, turn-of-the-twentieth-century design. The work was expensive and laborious and took six years to complete, but the investment paid off in a way unimagined. Years before, in its heyday, the Metropol had attracted the cream of Moscow society including writers, composers, singers, and actors such as Leo Tolstoy, Sergei Rachmaninov, and Feodor Shalyapin; now its five-star update with old-world atmosphere attracted Western pop stars, tourists, and businessmen, high-ranking political figures, and Russians with new money.

There was also a café in the Hotel Ukraine, just off the foyer. The coffee wasn't much but it was entertaining to watch the comings and goings of the Russian nouveau riche and their accompanying bodyguards. The Ukraine is a vast, brooding building across the river from the White House, and one of Stalin's famous wedding cake-designed buildings known as Seven Sisters. Others included the House of Writers and Moscow University on Sparrow Hills, overlooking the city—a spot often featured in movies as a meeting place for spies, because of the convenient parks, trees, wooden benches, and strolling people.

The Ministry of Foreign Affairs or MID was also housed in one of the Seven Sisters. MID controlled passports, visas, and the general movements of foreigners and was the one place where we did not want to be well known. Put one foot wrong and your embassy would hear from MID. They had the power to reject and eject diplomats, businessmen, and any other foreigners and often did.

Diane Mason and I tried the basement café of the Writers Union for coffee. The coffee was instant—Nescafé having been discovered—with canned milk, and we were soon joined by an alarming man who seemed to know all about us and about John's and Sam's work at the embassy. Having partnered our husbands in espionage, this wasn't good and we didn't go back. Only the wives of the Canadian, American, British, and to a lesser extent, the French and German military attachés were part of a team with their husbands. Looking back, I think it was extremely foolish of Canadian wives, unpaid as we were, to think the government would have supported us if we'd been caught undertaking some clandestine task in the host country. The GRU knew about the wives' involvement and were mildly amused. After all, we didn't wear SMERSH-approved shoes with knives in the toes. We were a smiley, friendly, sympathetic lot and I'm sure not a bit like the agents of that wartime Soviet counterintelligence agency sinisterly portrayed in James Bond movies.

Diane and I also discovered a restaurant on the fourteenth floor of the Hotel Moskva with similar-tasting coffee but by way of compensation, a good view of the city. We asked a waitress how we could reach a top-floor balcony we had seen from the square in front of the hotel and were told to exit via the kitchen and take a small elevator a few floors up. We emerged onto a balcony that not only laid the downtown at our feet, but also gave us a bird's-eye view over the Kremlin wall. We realized it was probably highly illegal for us to be there carrying the kind of identity we did, so didn't take photographs. When we took our husbands to the same restaurant and attempted to show them the way to the balcony our way was barred by kitchen staff. The balcony was forbidden to foreigners, they said, because it overlooked the seat of power. Apparently it had been okay for us because we were only women and presumably not a threat.

The Hotel Metropol was also my favourite place for eating Sunday lunch, but it was expensive and one could only afford to go there on special occasions. Once, lunching with a Russian woman, I watched an orthodox priest stuffing the pockets under his beard and black robes with extra food to take home. It was an expensive place for him to be in the first place. He was probably there to bless a "biznis" deal. Priests were being asked to bless everything with holy water—new shopping malls, luxury cars, and expensive houses. The woman sighed as she watched him shoving the good food into his mouth and pockets. She said, "We Russians have no brakes on excess."

9

Carpet Bagging

After the final collapse of the Soviet Union in December 1991 we started to visit territory that once had been closed or restricted to foreign visitors. Our job was to look around, talk to the locals, meet officials (military, ministers, mayors, and heads of industry), and report to Ottawa on how the new situation in that part of the world was evolving. Armies, weapons, people, oil, gas, agriculture, and major industries of the Soviet Union had all been divided among the new countries, and the West was interested in the consequences.

The security forces that had until recently been under the control of Moscow, now took their orders from new governments in new countries. But Sam was still a military attaché and they were still KGB. Nothing had changed—we were foreign spies under the existing rules and their job was to thwart our efforts. Perhaps our activities weren't quite as portrayed in movies or books—not enough action, our sleuthing a bit mundane. But the unpredictability of confronting the secret police in its own backyards generated real-life excitement.

Having Yeltsin at the helm of Russia during the division was a stroke of luck for the emerging states. A sober leader, someone less distracted by his dislike of his predecessor, might have carefully picked and chosen, keeping for Russia the rich oil fields of the Caspian, the picturesque and historic Crimea, and other strategic areas, and created new borders. The existing ones hadn't been very official in the first place. This would have caused unrest and conflict.

As it was, Yeltsin's old friends, also former high-ranking members of the Soviet Communist Party *apparatchik*, became presidents of the new Central Asian countries and began to behave like benevolent dictators, some more benevolent than others.

When we visited Turkmenistan in January 1992, it was too soon after the fall of the Soviet Union to know that the country's first and only president, Saparmurat Niyazov, would become the most authoritarian and repressive of all the Central Asian leaders. He adopted the title Turkmenbashi (great leader of Turkmen) in 1993 and in 1999 was proclaimed president for life.

In Soviet times, as in neighbouring Uzbekistan, cotton was Turkmenistan's major industry. But because the country is mostly desert, Soviet engineers built a 1,400-kilometre canal to bring water from the Amu-Darya River, on the Uzbek border, to irrigate the cotton fields. The canal, which was begun in the fifties and worked on through the sixties, seventies, and eighties, compounded the environmental tragedy of the Aral Sea.

Fortunately for Turkmenistan, it is one of the five littoral countries of the Caspian Sea—the others being Azerbaijan, Iran, Kazakhstan, and Russia—and it has access to offshore oil. The country also possesses oil deposits, as well as abundant natural gas resources, under the desert. But in early 1992, big western business had yet to arrive.

Although still winter, the weather was mild in the capital Ashgabat, situated on the edge of the Karakum Desert, and we did our usual walking tour of the city in light clothing. Ashgabat has existed under different guises for thousands of years, from when the area was first settled during the Parthian empire. Silk Road trading brought prosperity until the small town was destroyed by marauding Mongol hordes. Ashgabat enjoyed a revival in the late nineteenth century when it was chosen as the site of a wealthy Russian garrison. At the turn of the twentieth century the city was even attracting tourists.

But all of this history was lost in 1948 when Ashgabat was flattened by an earthquake that killed two-thirds of its population. The city was rebuilt by the Soviets according to their usual bland style. In 1992, Ashgabat seemed to have become a sleepy, ignored city, unlike go-ahead Tashkent. Fast-forward fourteen years and the booming oil and gas industry has added new hotels, government buildings, grand palaces, fountains, and monuments to the city's dusty streets.

The Intourist Ashgabat Hotel was not a pleasant habitat in the early nineties with its stained wallpaper, multitudes of large black cockroaches—the kind that can be caught in mousetraps—and indigestible food. The hotel provided us with a guide, who took us on a ten-kilometre drive west to the famous archaeological site of Nisa, the Parthian fortress city situated in the foothills of the Kopet Dag Mountains near the border with Iran. We had wanted to go east to a city called Mary that we knew had been home to a Soviet air force fighter base, but our guide said it was too far and anyway, we weren't allowed to go there.

All that was left of Nisa, razed by the Mongols in the thirteenth century, were a few grassy ridges and sand pits. We looked across at the mountains and asked if we could get a closer look at the border a few kilometres away. We wanted to see whether it was still being patrolled by Russian troops. "Sorry," the guide said firmly, the border area was out of bounds.

We seemed to be the only foreigners at the carpet bazaar outside Ashgabat on Sunday, but Turkmen were there in droves selling handwoven carpets and heirloom jewellery, antiques, traditional silk clothing, camels, and goats. The bazaar had taken on an even bigger significance now that the Soviet Union—the giant market place for the cotton industry—was no more.

The carpets were laid out on the desert floor in a walled compound. The women weavers sat crouched beside them, their red and maroon dresses matching the colours of the famous Turkmenistan traditional carpets. We stopped looking when we discovered, spread out on the sand, a dark red, wool, handwoven carpet in an intricate tribal design. The knots were tight and tied carefully. It stood out like a work of art and said, "buy me."

I knew that good carpets from Turkmenistan were prized. Afghanistan used to make some of the best in the region but the years of war and its aftermath have intervened; Afghan rugs are still being produced, but according to a carpet seller in Kazakhstan, many of the good Afghan makers have moved to bordering Central Asian countries such as Turkmenistan to pursue their craft. Azerbaijan carpets are also good, although shortly after 1991, the industry workers struggled to purchase the necessary dyes. Kazakhstan carpets are well made but more garish and folksy while the really prized carpets are made in neighbouring Iran.

The young woman sitting beside the carpet I was admiring lowered her eyes beneath her colourful scarf. She was reluctant to sell but was persuaded by her relatives to take the dollars we were offering. She had spent long hours on her work. Now, quicker than she liked, she had to give it up to some stranger. Her relatives were wiser. It was becoming harder to take their wares to Moscow and sell them there and no one was coming from Russia to buy. Who knew what the future would bring? The woman took our money but only grudgingly. She looked at it as if she had never seen American dollars before and was doubtful about their authenticity. We felt almost guilty buying her carpet.

10

Oil and Fire

It was the spring of 1992 before we visited Azerbaijan. Ironically we were still flying out of Russia to the republics as military attachés accredited to the Soviet Union; we hadn't yet been officially reassigned to the new countries. Only Russia had moved on the issue—in the new year its ministry of defence gathered all the foreign attachés together in Moscow and granted them instant re-accreditation. The Russian security service (its acronym had changed from KGB to FSK, but it remained pretty much the same) and GRU still directed much of what we did and where we went, whether it was in-country or in the new states.

The Soviet army had been broken up into fifteen separate armies and the weaponry divided up largely according to the rule of "whatever is in the republic is yours." The various ethnic military members were reassigned to protect their own homelands—Kazakhstanis defending Kazakhstan, Ukrainians defending the Ukraine, and so on. The Baltic republics were adamant that Russian soldiers should leave their soil immediately and a few diplomatic skirmishes occurred when the former Soviet army appeared to drag its feet over leaving some of its infrastructure behind and the ethnic Russian residents unprotected. But this was gradually resolved and one couldn't help but be amazed by the mostly amicable though unplanned division of forces and weapons (nuclear in Kazakhstan and Russia's case). It was a remarkable feat.

There was bloodshed, however, when some of the new countries started to flex their muscles. Azerbaijan had declared independence from the Soviet Union at the end of August 1991 and then in November abolished the autonomy of a region bordering Armenia called Nagorno-Karabakh. This move infuriated Armenia because, even though the enclave had been assigned to Muslim Azerbaijan by Moscow in the 1920s, it was mostly populated by Christian Armenians. In December 1991, the Armenian population of Nagorno-Karabakh declared independence from Azerbaijan. The new Azerbaijan army responded with force. A war ensued.

The conflict was at its height when we arrived in Baku, the capital of Azerbaijan.

We were shown to a room on the fourteenth floor of the Hotel Azerbaijan. What with the airport food and the barely passable fare on the planes, we were usually hungry when we arrived at any of our destinations. For that reason we carried items such as tins of corned beef, muesli, powdered milk, crackers, apples, tea, and mineral water. We knew we could probably get local bread and tomatoes to make a pleasant lunch. We always packed the same items for our away trips and had a checklist that we began to know by heart.

We had a breakfast of cereal, and went to boil water with our heating element for tea when we discovered our room had no electricity. We phoned the desk and were told it would be repaired later. So we went out to explore Baku.

Baku is called the "city of fire" because of the enormous quantities of oil and gas this Caspian Sea area contains. In ancient times the city was declared a holy site by fire-worshippers from Persia (Iran) because of the flames that sprouted through rocky ground, fed by hidden oil and gas deposits. For hundreds of years from the seventh century, Baku was a trading centre for silk and spices from

India, Afghanistan, and Iran. The narrow cobbled streets, fortress walls, mosques, and caravanserais (ancient inns) from that period still exist in the Old Town. An oil boom in the late nineteenth century bought western companies flocking to Baku and rich industrialists built mansions in the city. Then after the Russian Revolution of 1905, Baku became the major supplier of oil to Moscow and the city was given a Soviet look.

However, our first impression was of an environmental disaster. How many disaster areas could there be in the former Soviet Union? Perhaps two-thirds of the place if you count the nuclear, industrial, agricultural, mining, oil, and gas areas. The Soviets hadn't paid any attention to the environment at all and our Intourist bus in Baku took us past field after field covered in black oil spills.

Later, on a walk along the city's promenade, the oily Caspian Sea rolled up to the beach in an apologetic black wave. We took a boat ride out to the oil derricks just offshore. I didn't like our chances of survival if the boat sank in those dark oily waters. I don't think the environment has improved that much since, despite the new oil boom in Azerbaijan and the huge influx of foreign investment over the past fourteen years. On a recent plane ride over Baku I could still see the oily streaks leading from the derricks to the coastline.

When we returned to the hotel, the electricity still wasn't working. Sam demanded another room. This was an irregular demand as the room had probably been specially prepared for an attaché guest and although the Soviet Union was no more, we assumed the country still had active security police and listeners would be in place. But Sam insisted and shortly afterwards we were told to take our belongings to the eleventh floor.

As it turned out the new room was at the end of the building overlooking the port. Military attachés weren't usually allowed views from hotel windows of "strategic locations" so we took advantage of the situation and shot numerous photos before we went downstairs to see if there was anything to eat in the restaurant.

It would also give our friends time to fix up the bugs in the new room. It was only fair.

We never really unpacked our bags except for the clothes we wanted to put on the next day. So when we were awakened in the early morning by frantic knocking we just slipped into our trousers and shirts before calling, "What do you want?" It was five in the morning and still dark outside. At first we thought it was KGB harassment.

The knocking grew more frantic. It was a man's voice that called, "Open your door." It must have been serious or the knocker would have relied on the woman who looked after the floor to wake us. We opened the door. Outside in the hall stood a very worried Azerbaijani. He could have been a member of the security service, because keeping an eye on us also meant looking after us. He said, "There's a fire. Please bring your money, jewels, and wife and come downstairs." In that order. And it wasn't part of a game—we could smell smoke.

With no jewels to worry about, we grabbed our jackets (containing our money and passports), our two carry bags and, being Canadian, our toothbrushes from the bathroom. The man waited outside in the hall for the few seconds it took. We followed him to the stairs. There was water everywhere on the stairs and leaky hoses leading upwards. Firefighters were already at work above us.

Outside it seemed we were the last guests to leave. Perhaps in the confusion the desk had forgotten we had changed our rooms. But it was fortunate that we had. When we reached the road and looked up, we could see seven-metre flames shooting up from the fourteenth floor. From the very room that we had occupied the day before. Perhaps someone had tried to fix the electricity and failed.

We watched for a while as a firefighter tried to fight the fire from a ladder that was refusing to reach higher than the twelfth floor, swaying backwards and forwards. The firefighter was having enough trouble holding on, let alone hosing the fire.

All the guests from the hotel were gathered there and after taking a few photographs of the scene, it dawned on us that the Hotel

Azerbaijan would not be open for business anymore that day. It was too smoke and water damaged. We waved to a passing car and it immediately turned into a taxi. Is there another hotel in the area? The driver nodded and drove off with us, climbing a hill above the city. It was a brand new hotel. The owner and staff were standing outside. We went in with our bags like flies into a web.

"How much for a room?"

"Eighty dollars."

The Intourist price for diplomats was about fifteen dollars, but there wasn't much we could do. We needed a place to sleep and the man was not going to budge. We agreed and were shown to our room. Immediately we discovered there was no water in either of the taps. The management said, "Oh, you want water? That'll be ninety dollars." The water was contained in two large bottles. Fortunately, we had drinking water with us, so we could use both bottles for showering. Apparently, although oil was in plentiful supply in Baku, drinking water was a precious commodity.

This time our room overlooked a sombre scene: a cemetery for the dead from the war in Nagorno-Karabakh. Even as we watched, an open truck drew up containing a body wrapped in a white cloth and a host of Azerbaijani male mourners (females did their mourning at home). That day, wandering through the cemetery looking at all the freshly dug graves, we witnessed two more burials.

We hadn't yet fulfilled our customary visits to government sites such as KGB headquarters and military barracks We decided to climb the brick Maiden Tower in the old town that afforded a good view of the city. By the time we reached the top we had two minders with us and didn't take any photographs. One of the two men came up to us and said, "Would you like me to take a photo of you both with your camera?" We declined politely.

That day we had our first meeting with a representative from the former Soviet army, a colonel in the new Azerbaijan military. The meeting had been arranged of course by the military liaison office in Moscow and the discussion mainly centred on the war in Nagorno-Karabakh. A smoothly handsome Azeri, the colonel pleaded for Canada's understanding of the conflict from his country's point of view. Sam said he would let Ottawa know.

We heard the opposing view on the disputed enclave when we flew into Armenia while the war was still being grimly fought. The wounds were still deep and bleeding when we arrived in Yerevan, Armenia's capital.

At the same time the country was undergoing a severe fuel shortage. The evidence was obvious—the locals had cut down all the trees lining the city's avenues and streets to heat their homes. One couple told us they lit their fires on the apartment's wooden floor and cracked open the window a little to let out the smoke

Canada's honorary consul for Armenia met us at the airport. He was in his twenties, a Fulbright scholar, and was leaving the following year to study in America. His remarks were a downer: I wasn't allowed to go to the war zone with Sam because local officials considered it to be too dangerous. Also the religious aspect to the war made women unwelcome, and ..."We don't have room in the car."

He went on the journey to Nagorno-Karabakh with my husband and informed me that I would spend my day touring the city and surrounding area.

The men left at six in the morning in a Zhiguli, and a few hours later I was taken by a guide to see a nearby flea market (hurriedly getting out of the way of a knife fight between two local men). I was also taken to historic Echmiadzin Cathedral, which was about seven kilometres from Yerevan and which had been built over a pagan temple in the fourth century. It just so happened that on the day I visited, sheep and lambs were being slaughtered in the inner courtyard in what I was told by our guide was a pagan sacrifice.

Meanwhile Sam was on his way to Nagorno-Karabakh and it was a tough ride. Five hours there and five hours back through mountain passes and along steep hilly roads with sheer drops. The hired driver drove fast but when the honorary consul took over the wheel after three hours, he increased the speed even more. They drove through war-torn towns and small villages and passed burned-out Azeri tanks and armoured personnel carriers as they neared the capital of the region, Stepanakert. Among the rubble, children could be seen lining up for school.

Their meeting was with Robert Kocharian, then leader of Nagorno-Karabakh, now president of Armenia. He insisted that the war was between the ethnic Armenians living in Nagorno-Karabakh and Azerbaijan, not Armenia and Azerbaijan.

To view a conflict and discuss it in earnest with both sides in countries that used to be part of the Soviet Union was something new for a western military attaché. This was a sign that things were changing; our days of creeping around on foot and public transport might soon be over. Doors were opening and we were to be given firsthand information.

It wasn't our job to take sides or be judgmental. Nor could we be. We weren't experts. But we were genuinely interested and listened sympathetically to both the Azerbaijanis and Armenians we met, passing on the information to Canada.

We continued to enjoy our unique career. As for Nagorno-Karabakh, although the dispute is still not completely settled, a ceasefire has been in effect for some time.

11

Spies' Lies

It was a good time to be a spy. At the height of the Cold War, many of the trips we were taking would have been fraught with tension and danger rather than adventure. During the year following the 1991 coup, no one knew what might happen next politically; were we to be treated as friends or enemies? Was it okay to tell us everything or nothing?

The so-called secret cities, the scientific laboratories, the aircraft factories, and the experimental programs had all become so run down through lack of money that they needed support to go on—anybody's support. They wanted to see us as people who could help them. Perhaps when we took our tales back to Ottawa someone might say, "That's a brilliant idea. Let's form a joint venture." And as for our minders, perhaps they saw us less as the enemy and more as conduits to jobs with western companies.

What they didn't realize right away, though they soon caught on, was that nothing had changed as far as the West was concerned. We were still there to find out as much as we could. We weren't planning to help them, just ourselves. It was a wonderful window for building some trust and turning their suddenly upside-down world the right way up by doing genuine business, but we missed the opportunity. Instead, we gave them off-target, untested economic advice and supported ten years of the struggling Yeltsin. We watched as oligarchs grabbed the best of what was available, as IMF money disappeared into overseas accounts, and as foreign embassies stamped "immigration granted" on the passports of the best brains as they drained out of the country.

The scientists of Academgorodok in Siberia had been left in limbo by the collapse of the Soviet Union. A former closed city about a hundred kilometres from Novosibirsk, Academgorodok had been one of Russia's most important scientific centres. For years, brilliant, well-paid men and women had worked in wooden buildings set in a circle among picturesque white birch trees, concentrating on keeping the Soviet Union's science ahead of the West's.

When we visited the area in the early summer of 1992, the laboratories that had once hummed with the brainpower of scientists working on government secret projects were quiet. Professors, who before would have been scared to talk to us, were eager to discuss their work. Their standard of living had plummeted. There was no money for them or their programs. They just wanted a weekly pay cheque and were prepared to work hard for it. Could we tell our people back in Canada that there were possibilities for joint ventures on new inventions and projects already successfully tested?

I was amazed and a little perturbed by how sincere, trusting, and seemingly gullible these clever people were. They were desperate but we had a job to do and we had to lie to them in their faces. It was the worst part of our spying then. The people we worked for weren't interested in the plight of these people. Only in the fact that all was shut down, nothing was working.

I could have written human-interest stories about them for newspapers, but I was in places where I was only allowed because of my diplomatic status. One story and that would have been the end of it. We listened to these clever people, most of them very senior, wearing shabby, but probably their best, suits. We told them, as

I scribbled in a pad, that we would tell the Canadian government about their projects, their unique inventions, successful experiments, and practical achievements and we assured them that there would be great interest.

These people weren't asking to defect: they didn't want to leave their country. They just wanted to continue to work. They were desperate. We said that Canadian companies would surely be interested in joint ventures. Give us all the details, we said, and we would pass them on. They were open and honest; we weren't. We gave them promises and hinted at visits and exchanges. But in the meantime, could we please have all the information about their products? Of course we passed everything on to Ottawa. But we knew that helping to better the lives of these extraordinary people just wasn't part of the agenda.

Everyone did it, including the Brits, the Americans, the French, and the Germans: extracting information about new projects from factory heads, inventors, and academics, then later turning it into their own use. I don't think it was cruelty; the West was so used to getting facts the hard way, they didn't know how to handle the immense turnabout of getting so much information in good faith.

But the Russian scientific community quickly woke up to the brutal truth of the competitive market economy and soon slammed the window of cooperation shut. Who could blame them?

12

Shadowy Journalists

In August 1992 I started working as an editor on a brand-new, English-language newspaper in Moscow. I had to get permission from Ottawa to do this work, or at least let them know. But they didn't really say yes and they didn't say no. Head spies were short on making any sort of commitment when it came to direction in the field, I was learning. Perhaps it was understandable. The rules of the game were all new. A military attaché's wife working on a Russian-owned newspaper? It would have been unthinkable during the Cold War. If Ottawa had objected I would have tried to sell them the idea that it was a great place to pick up information. Maybe that thought had already occurred to them.

I had seen an advertisement for editors and reporters for the *Moscow Tribune* in a British Embassy news bulletin that Sam brought home in May 1992. I arranged to meet with the newspaper's publisher. In June I sat down with twenty-four-year-old Anthony Louis, creator of the *Tribune*, in his office at 45 Leninsky Prospekt.

"How would you describe Anthony?" I was asked by someone thinking of coming to work for the paper. I said, "A teddy bear." But although he had a cuddly look, being too rotund for a twenty-something, and had a boyish smile, he was often socially inept at handling his peers (especially expats) and was too tough on them. It wasn't Anthony's fault; it was the result of his interesting English-Russian background, an encyclopaedic brain that demanded perfection, and a sense of humour that young people couldn't always fathom.

He was tall enough to stoop slightly when speaking to someone my height (five foot one) and favoured Harry Palmer-type spectacles. Already balding, his crumpled grey, hand-knitted cardigan (that would become his office uniform), open-necked white shirt, and grey trousers (if he wore jeans they sagged), made him appear older than his years. With me he laughed easily, comfortable in the presence of elders.

He resembled a *Times* reporter I had known in London and just to make conversation I asked him if his father had been a journalist. Anthony laughed at that as he assumed I knew who his father was, diplomats being such gossips. But I didn't know about his father then. Anthony had an English sense of humour and we got along. I agreed that I would work as an editor on his newspaper to be launched later that summer, and he said he would be in touch within a month.

I found out a lot about Anthony's father before I saw him again because he died in a London hospital during the third week of July and his death was reported in *Time Magazine*'s prestigious Milestones column. Several years before *Time* had described Victor Louis as "a favourite KGB conduit for slipping information to the West," in regards to a story about dissident physicist Andrei Sakharov. In Milestones, *Time* referred to him as "that shadowy figure, Victor Louis." Anthony was his youngest son.

The Masons were eager to fill me in. They said Victor Louis had been the object of much gossip and speculation in diplomatic and journalistic circles, especially at the Canadian, American, and British embassies.

It was widely believed that during the Cold War, Louis' job for the KGB was to feed stories, true and false, to the western media.

This was easy for him, since the press was eager for news from inside the Soviet Union. Louis' critics argued that his KGB job also entailed being on the lookout for likely western journalists to recruit. But he had his supporters. They figured the man had paid his dues—he had spent ten years in a gulag just for the crime of working for a foreign embassy in the forties. He was only released after Stalin's death. Sympathizers both Russian and foreign felt he had provided a service to the western press during the years of Soviet secrecy. While he must have fed some things back to the Kremlin in order to survive he had also used the KGB for his own purposes.

I was fascinated by Victor Louis. I felt it was unfortunate that I'd never had a chance to meet him since. Apart from being drawn to infamy, especially the spying kind, I had heard that though he could be aloof, his sense of humour made him good company. He certainly made times exciting for diplomats and journalists during the Cold War and they eagerly accepted invitations to his large *dacha*. In return, Louis was a guest at many embassy functions.

Louis and his family lived at Bakovka, a settlement outside of Moscow where senior Soviet officials had summer homes. It bordered on Peredelkino, an exclusive writers' colony where Russian literary giants such as Nobel Prize winner Boris Pasternak, author of *Dr. Zhivago*, lived and died. He also had a large apartment in downtown Moscow, where the *Moscow Tribune* would eventually be located.

A tall, solid security fence surrounded the Louis' impressive wooden dacha; a bell at the access gate summoned a guard. Just inside the gate to the right stood a large garage in which had been parked during the Cold War years several personal vehicles including a Peugeot, a Porsche, a Land Rover and a Rolls-Royce, some at the same time. It was rumoured that packages were hand delivered to his dacha, mailed from overseas and addressed simply to "Victor Louis, The Kremlin, Moscow."

This was long before the advent of the New Russians with their grandiose homes, bodyguards, and fast foreign cars. Only certain people with friends in high places were able to acquire such items in the sixties, seventies, and even the eighties.

There were only three people in the Soviet Union with a Rolls-Royce—Louis, Brezhnev, and the British Ambassador to Moscow. Anthony told me that one day his father called the ambassador to ask if he could use his car jack—his had broken and he needed one right away. (His wife, Jennifer, was English after all and a stalwart member of the Anglican Church and the International Women's Club.) After a pause Louis was told, "No, I'm sorry. If I lend you mine everyone will want to borrow it!"

A close friend of another controversial figure, media mogul Robert Maxwell, Louis wrote for a score of publications including *France Soir, Yedioth Ahoronot* (Israel), some Australian papers, and the *Washington Post*. From the mid-fifties he was accredited by the USSR Foreign Ministry as Moscow correspondent for the *London Evening News*. When that paper closed he wrote for the *London Evening Standard* and was a correspondent for Maxwell's *Sunday Express*.

The Russian television station NTV, which now broadcasts in the US, did a one-hour show on Victor in 2002, which featured a man in the shadows, supposedly the spy himself, talking about his life. Anthony told me it was horrible and badly written. It would have been incredible if NTV had got the facts right because Victor Louis had a reputation for never revealing the real truth to anybody, his family included.

It was understandable that after the sudden death of his father I didn't hear from Anthony again until early August 1992. Then, after a brief meeting of the newly hired editorial staff—three reporters, a sports editor, a news editor, a photographer, and me, the editor—we began work on our first edition that finally came out in early September. From the outset, diplomats and foreign business people in Moscow liked our newspaper because we had so many reports by Russian insiders. Being locally owned it had a Russian point of view. However, because Anthony was the son of Victor Louis, diplomats would often ask me, "What is the ideological view of your newspaper?"

Anyone who had seen the editors and writers—the staff quickly doubled and then quadrupled in size—putting the finishing touches to our thirty-page daily at one in the morning would have realized there was no time for ideology. Our rival, the *Moscow Times*, owned by Independent Media, a Dutch company, had more money and constantly poached our staff. In some ways you couldn't blame the defectors. The *Tribune* was constantly struggling because of money flow, and gave up life as a daily six or seven years after its ambitious 1992 start. For a while it continued as a weekly and then it faded away.

But there was an air of camaraderie and dedication at the *Tribune* that I wouldn't have swapped for the world, even though Anthony, a stickler for accuracy, drove us all mad—especially late at night when a new story broke on our deadline. We had to include the new lead however late it kept us. Then he would chant in Russian and English, "Check the date, check the edition number, check spellings (especially transliterations), check punctuation, check the advertisements," as he moved among the editors and designers. He had two personalities—diplomatic Englishman and outspoken Russian. I reaped the benefits of the former while the local and younger expat staff suffered the latter. No wonder then, that I could add "teddy" to their "bear" in describing him.

Given my other life as an intelligence gatherer, I found our Russian correspondents and opinion columnists most intriguing. The latter included ex-KGB heads, current political biggies, scientists, and former generals in the Soviet army. The world had turned topsy-turvy—instead of my having to listen at keyholes and peer over "attaché fences" to collect clandestine photos and information, it was all marching into my office and being laid out on my desk. I could hardly contain my excitement at some of the photos—arrays of missiles, the latest fighter jets, new helicopters—that military attachés were still struggling to capture. I vaguely remembered some ethical code about spying and journalism, but if there were any ethics between the two in Russia in the early nineties, they were only in my head.

For the first few months of working as an editor on the *Moscow Tribune* I walked to the Kievskaya metro station from our apartment every morning. I passed by the hut of the three or four men who "guarded" our compound and always gave them a wave. I walked down eight-lane Bolshaya Dorogomilovskaya Street, past a hardware store Canadian residents called "Canadian Tiresky," and crossed at the traffic lights prior to Borodinsky Bridge along with hundreds of other Muscovites.

Small stalls set up by entrepreneurs on city streets following the fall of Communism created more and more of an obstacle course. Outside the hardware store they sold exactly the same items as inside, only just a few kopeks cheaper. One had to wonder where they got the stuff.

There was a popular bakery on the other side of the lights and some days I stopped to buy bread for lunch. There were always line-ups and they could be intimidating. Any deliberation on bread choice would be greeted with exasperated sighs from shop assistants and other customers alike. But the bread was worth any derision— it smelled delicious and was. The dark bread was more popular with Russians than with me. I liked the doughy white variety, but it didn't remain fresh for more than a day and was best eaten warm.

I crossed another road into the market area just before the station. Everything was for sale, including food, clothes, drink, and cigarettes. One hazard just before the heavy swinging doors into the metro station was the beggars. Attracting their attention was not a good idea. Never look too bright, cheery, foreign, or approachable was the rule. Always look grim and determined and keep walking no matter who is holding onto your arm or leg. No one ever bothered me, but there were many instances of foreign women being swarmed by street children and losing everything that could be lifted.

Moscow's metro is very efficient. Trains arrive at two-minute intervals or less. There might have been rats playing between the rails, but because of the fast schedule one didn't have too much time to observe them. As for cleanliness, it compares very favourably to London's.

People in general feel completely safe on the metro. I rode it regularly between 1991 and 1994, again for a year in 1996, and then in 1998 and 2002. At all hours, women of all ages embarked and disembarked fearlessly. I am sure the city streets aren't quite as safe today but on the whole Moscow men don't prey on women walking alone as they do in Europe (especially the UK where one doesn't feel safe walking down any lonely road, even in daylight) and North America. It may be something to do with the way boys are brought up by their mothers and grandmothers, or even Communism, under which everyone worked and was equal.

I changed to another train at Park Kultury station, where one descends at quite a fast pace into the bowels of the earth. The stations were always bustling and the masses carried me along from one rail line to the next. In rush hour I just concentrated on going in the right direction and tried not to be distracted by an old man watching his dropped groceries being scattered by flying feet, or an old lady trying to sweep the stairs. The train headed down Leninsky Prospekt to Leninsky station, not much more than half a kilometre from the newspaper office.

During World War Two, the stations were used as underground shelters for Moscow's twelve million inhabitants, in the same way that London's underground served its population. Some of Moscow's metro stations are tourist attractions in their own right—

airy halls decorated with colourful mosaics and life-sized bronze statues. It's best not to be too observant though when on the train. I frightened myself once while riding in the front carriage and happened to look out of the window down the track. As far as the eye could see I only saw red lights that we hurtled past at breakneck speed. I just hoped the driver knew something that I didn't.

Eventually, when I was familiar with the route and Moscow's traffic, I drove my own little red Lada to work and I parked it on the street under the office window. The car was bought from a gathering of about fifteen or sixteen Russian men standing around a couple of cars in a parking lot in downtown Moscow, and cost me $3,500 US. My husband had previously exchanged the dollars for thousands of roubles, which he'd stuffed inside a sports bag. The wheeling and dealing was done inside the vehicle. Two men took the cash and stuffed it inside their shirts, as they handed over the keys to the car. Then they said they were going to get the vehicle's documents.

It was like an exchange of spies at a border crossing, said my husband. No one knew who to trust and who would make the first move. After a short while the men returned and gave Sam some papers. Miraculously they seemed in order and soon the car was licensed and registered by the authorities and I received a Russian driving licence based on my Canadian one.

The car helped me get home safely when I had to work until the early hours of the morning, but seeing the odd stiff body of what I assumed was a drunk pedestrian, the victim of a hit-and-run, lying on the road during the journey home was the downside. I could never understand why the victim's shoes were always so neatly placed together on the side as if he had just stepped out of them. I would like to say that I stopped but I didn't, I just wove my way around the body with the rest of the traffic.

Although I worked full time as a newspaper editor I was still obliged to entertain several times a month: foreign diplomats,

Russian military chiefs, politicians, cultural figures, and visiting senior military from Canada. On the nights we were entertaining I usually arrived home about six o'clock for the arrival of guests at eight. The entertaining of Russian dignitaries, only possible after 1991, was the best part of the deal. I was able to find out some answers to news stories that puzzled me, which served both the paper and my diplomatic obligations. I also continued travelling with Sam.

13

Shooting Stars

The job at the *Moscow Tribune* was one reason I spent so much of our first trip to Kazakhstan writing travel stories. I had to justify my being away from the office. It fitted in because taking sightseeing side trips was all part of the work of being a spy.

Alma Ata, now known as Almaty, could at first glance have been mistaken for a city nestled in the Rocky Mountains or the Swiss Alps. But during the drive from the airport, we noticed missing manhole covers, one-storey wooden homes, and shabby concrete apartment blocks, reminding us that we were in the recently collapsed Soviet Union. Factories belched smoke and buses emitted fumes that cast a pall of pollution over the city. But it hovered there because of the way Almaty nestled in the lee of the mountains. Still, there were plenty of healthy, tall oak trees lining the streets, and roses still blooming alongside the boulevards.

Alma Ata means "Father of Apples," and there were numerous fruit orchards to be found on the outskirts of the city. In the fall of 1992, there were no five-star hotels, no presidential palace or shopping mall, and only one or two restaurants deemed passable for foreigners. (In 2006, Almaty is a sophisticated business centre celebrating its new economic clout with the construction of the tallest building in Central Asia—a 38-storey luxury hotel, residential, business and fitness complex.)

In Soviet times, Almaty's sanatoriums had been considered a haven of rest for Communist leaders and their cronies. The city boasted a skating rink that had trained Soviet Olympic speed skaters. Above the rink towered a huge dam, built to protect the city against mudslides and avalanches. Up higher, among clean skies, a four-kilometre, three-stage chair lift put skiers (in the winter) and walkers (in the summer) at the foot of a spectacular glacier.

We had a meeting planned with the new chief of the Kazakhstan Armed Forces. He was Kazakh, and a former Soviet general. Once again we were invited in through the front door to talk to the military. Perhaps this access would produce more facts and less guesswork. These were still new times for former USSR generals, and it must have been difficult to adapt to meeting western military attachés on a friendly basis. They still didn't trust us of course, and that was fine with us. A year after the breakup who knew what was going to happen next? Kazakhstan had been left with a share of the Soviet's nuclear capability just because of its physical location. Our job was to try to find out what the new Kazakhstan military was going to do with this dangerous legacy.

Later it would became clear that right from the start huge, landlocked Kazakhstan wanted to be rid of the problems associated with owning nuclear weapons and, aided by the US, quickly disposed of them. It fully intended to steer a path from Communism to market reform and was helped by the numerous western investors who flocked to develop its oil, gas, and mining resources. The country has suffered its share of crime and corruption, but generally it has stayed the course towards democracy. Only one power resource suffered—brains—as thousands of ethnic Russians, Germans, Ukrainians, and other Caucasians, who had been teachers, scientists, and business people, left. The Germans, descendants of those deported by Stalin to Kazakhstan before, during, and after the war had an invitation of repatriation from Germany, an offer most couldn't refuse. The Russians, who under Soviet rule had had the best jobs, the good promotions, and the preferred schooling in Kazakhstan—treating Kazakhs as second-class citizens—weren't going to stay around to endure payback time.

But here we were in Kazakhstan on that fall day, among the first attachés invited to tour the headquarters of a border guard regiment, to have lunch with the officers, to sit and talk to the chief about what he thought Canada could do for his border guards, his armed forces, and Kazakhstan in general. He was very well spoken and clearly bemused that we were having the talk at all. After all, his men had just followed us around the town as we made our trips past the KGB, the television tower, the radio station, the Orthodox church, and the war memorial.

I took notes at all of our meetings—I was the experienced interviewer after all—in a shorthand I had devised over the years, and then Sam forwarded the most important bits to military intelligence in Ottawa. When interviewees suggested that something might help them down the struggling path towards democracy the suggestion was never given a second thought or acted upon in any way, at least, not to my knowledge. Perhaps we were out of the loop on any follow-up, but likely we would have been informed to relieve us of the feeling that we were creating false hopes, that in order to get information we were telling white lies ("our government can help"), the way a desperate reporter might do to get a story ("my paper can help").

We always found one common ground when talking to former Soviet military and that was of course the Second World War. We were all on the same side then. The general told us that he had been in the Red Army when it had captured Berlin.

The next day, the Canadian embassy staff arranged for us to be taken on a tour into the mountains by Volkswagen bus. Almaty's Tien Shen mountain range has now been visited by countless foreign business people and adventure-seeking travellers, and the world has been made aware of Kazakhstan because of its oil and mineral riches and the publicity surrounding the woes of nearby Afghanistan. But in 1992 we were among the first foreign visitors to take advantage of the country's fledgling tourist industry.

The bus was old but not bad, and we set off up the mountain. It took us about thirty minutes to reach the snow line along a rutted dirt track that wound its way from the city to Little Almatinsky Lake. We could have been in the Rocky Mountains: the views were of high white peaks, green firs, and trailing white clouds against blue skies. The Tien Shen range contains three of the seven highest mountains in the world, and our driver and two escorts told us they had climbed most of the peaks in the range.

We hadn't seen another vehicle on the track. We stopped at a station that controlled the ice-cold mountain water gushing down a pipeline to Almaty for drinking. It stood innocuously just off the side of the road on a curve, but there was something about the low-slung concrete buildings that caught my attention. Only a few of the buildings were in use. Most of the others were derelict and trashed but built very much like barracks. Why? Was it a gulag from some time in the past? Our tour guides were puzzled by our interest. We got them to ask at the waterworks and discovered it had been a Japanese POW camp until the sixties. That's all they knew. It had been deserted since then. We took time to walk about the buildings and in some of the cell-like rooms found the remains of large rusted keys on the ground. It was exciting for us, a bit of history, but boring for the guides who wanted to show us the mountains not abandoned buildings.

The next part of the journey was hair-raising as the van clawed its way over muddy and snowy ruts, never very far from the edge of a drop. Then on a mountain ridge overlooking a turquoise lake we stopped. The three men bustled about erecting a table complete with tablecloth for our lunch. Ankle deep in snow, they rapidly cooked scrambled eggs, and we ate them with tomatoes and fresh bread. There was a drop of vodka to celebrate the tour and a bit of toasting. In the clean air, the refreshments went down well.

As our hosts cleaned up we wandered off to explore. Climbing higher and turning a corner we were surprised by a wire fence. On the other side were buildings. As spies there was only one thing to do: climb through the fence. The larger building was obviously an observatory, and as we approached it a man, an ethnic Russian, came towards us.

These were the early days of Kazakhstan's independence, and friendship with westerners was still new, but the man was welcoming and friendly. He probably led a rather lonely existence. "Do you want me to show you around?" he asked in Russian.

He took us into the observatory that was almost filled by a huge telescope. Before we were allowed a look through, he showed us slides of the many beautiful images he had captured as he observed the skies. He was obviously proud of his collection and started to shower a selection on us. We were reluctant at first, but he forced us to take at least half a dozen slides.

Then we came to the surprise. The telescope wasn't just any old magnifying instrument. The former Soviet scientist told us that Hitler had commissioned the telescope for his friend Mussolini. It had fallen into Red Army hands during the Second World War and been transported back to the Soviet Union. Now it sat on top of a mountain in Kazakhstan.

In 1993 we returned to Kazakhstan and tried out the original Soviet-built three-stage ski lift near Almaty in the area called Chimbulak. (Now there are new lifts at Chimbulak worthy of any European ski resort.) We were with the new Canadian ambassador to the region, Jeremy Kinsman and his wife, Hana. It was late summer, and they wanted to view the glacier. A man at the bottom of the lift said it wasn't working: it was under repair and dangerous. The ambassador offered him twenty dollars, and the lift suddenly started to move. There was one small kitchen-type chair per person about ten yards apart. Some were completely broken, slats and safety chains missing. Others weren't so bad. Through limited choice, our group, which also included our son Charles and his girlfriend, Miranda, was strung out over the mountain. The last time I looked back at the ambassador I saw him sitting sidewise on a chair with his legs over the arm. Since there was no snow to cushion anyone's fall and we were sailing fifty to seventy feet above rocks I wondered how we would explain losing Canada's high representative in an accident. But Jeremy seemed happy enough even though the chairs shuddered and swayed unnervingly as they passed under each supporting pylon.

When we visited Kazakhstan, we always tried to fit in a trip to Kyrgyzstan about 300 kilometres south of Almaty. Further away from Russia and therefore European influences, Kyrgyzstan is more underdeveloped than its neighbour and doesn't have the abundant oil and gas of Kazakhstan. It does have gold in large quantities and other minerals, however.

Besides the Tien Shen mountain range, Kyrgyzstan's major attraction is Lake Issyk-Kul, the second highest lake in the world. It used to be a drawing card for military attachés. Besides being a major tourist resort during Soviet times, the lake was also used for testing military equipment, in particular torpedoes for nuclear submarines. Consequently much of the lake was out of bounds to foreigners. The Russians possessed (and still do) one of the world's fastest and most effective torpedoes. It was one reason the doomed submarine *Kursk* was the centre of so much underwater surveillance by foreign navies during its ill-fated exercise in the Barents Sea.

On one occasion we drove to Kyrgyzstan with the adventurous Ambassador Kinsman when he had to present his Canadian credentials to the country's president. We drove in a two-car convoy that sped down the winding highway across the steppes at 200 kilometres per hour ignoring other traffic. We did these high-speed convoy drives several times as spies in the former Soviet Union, the scariest being between Grozny, Chechnya, and Vladikavkaz, Northern Ossetia. We also did them in Moscow and St. Petersburg with visiting dignitaries from Canada and with hosting local officials. In the city, the drives were official with flags flying. In the republics they were more low key, with the state-employed drivers just assuming they were carrying someone special and therefore must go very fast.

On another drive to Kyrgyzstan with just Sam, me, and a driver, we had reached the Bishkek city limits when we were pulled over by three *militsia* in a small Lada. We were in a black Mercedes. The police examined the driver's credentials and then wanted the trunk opened. They searched through our possessions and extracted a small bag that looked like it might contain valuable personal items. They opened the glove compartment and patted their way through looking for a weapon and then asked to see our passports.

It was when they kept the passports and asked us all to step out onto the sidewalk that I realized that something was not quite right. They asked us to accompany them to their office, and they pointed towards a dark alley. (It was after 10 P.M.) If I hadn't been tired after the drive I would have clued in before. I decided to go the route of a brusque Russian babushka. "Thank you, give me back my passport," I said, snatching it back. "I am going to sit in the car, and then I am going to call the president to complain." Our driver looked ashen at my remarks; he thought I had gone mad. Sitting in the back of the vehicle, I waited for Sam to see the light. He did, immediately, and said to the highwaymen, "Show me your ID." And when there was no ID forthcoming, "Give me back my passport." He also snatched back our bags. Fortunately, the three bandits were flabbergasted. Our driver hurried around and got in, and we drove off at high speed. We were shaken afterwards when we thought what might have happened.

Janice Cowan in Leningrad (now St. Petersburg) just prior to the fall of the Soviet Union.

Red Square, Moscow in the early nineties. St. Basil's Cathedral in the foreground and the Kremlin flying the new Russian flag in the background.

The glittering Bell Tower of Ivan the Great is the highest structure among the historic cathedrals, churches, and palaces in the Moscow Kremlin.

Visiting Canadian delegations were usually taken to see the Cathedral of the Assumption inside the walled monastery at Zagorsk (now Sergiev Posad), one of Russia's most important and historical landmarks about 60 kilometres from Moscow.

The Kremlin wall beside the Moscow River. On the opposite bank is the 19th century Kharitonenko mansion that, for 70 years, housed the British Embassy.

The Lenin Mausoleum stands by the Kremlin wall in Red Square. In the early nineties there were still lineups to view Lenin's waxy, preserved body.

Soviet tanks line up beside St. Basil's Cathedral in Red Square during the 1991 coup d'état (left) and surround the Kremlin (below).

Protesters manned barricades in front of the Russian White House for three days until the 1991 coup d'état was finally declared over and Gorbachev returned to Moscow.

The 1991 coup d'etat is over and all that remains in front of the White House in Moscow are the barricades of defiant protesters.

Soviet soldiers were armed and dangerous until the obvious collapse of the 1991 coup d'état.

A Soviet soldier relaxes during the coup d'état. He and his comrades have already joined Yeltsin's side.

People mill about the burned-out buses used as barricades by protesters during the 1991 coup d'état.

Mangled wreckage of a bus involved in an enounter with protesters and Russian tankists during the 1991 coup d'état.

A Soviet tankist discusses the exit route out of Moscow after the collapse of the 1991 coup d'état on the third day.

The 1991 coup d'état is doomed when Muscovites appear fearless in face of the Soviet Army's might.

Above left: Suzdal school children have some of the richest treasures of Russian national culture—centuries-old churches, cathedrals, convents, and monasteries—in their backyard.

Above right: A babushka on a snowy Moscow street. Desperate for money, some pensioners sold the contents of their homes on the sidewalks following the collapse of the Soviet Union.

Left: Russian children in the early nineties. They faced a future unimagined by their parents.

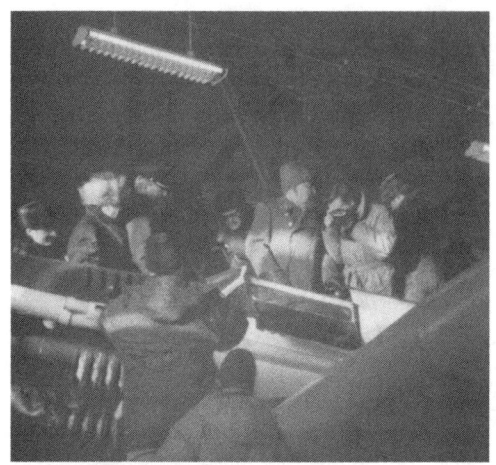

Ninety-six-year-old George Baidukov shows off the Tupolev ANT-25, the plane he co-piloted on an historic flight from Moscow to Washington State in 1937.

The 400-year-old Novodevichy Convent on the banks of the Moscow River.

Author Janice Cowan and some Russian geese brave the cold weather outside a 16th century monastery in Suzdal.

Inside the Intercession Convent in Suzdal where visitors can stay in small chalet-type izbas and eat breakfast in the refectory (above).

The historic walled monastery at Zagorsk (now Sergiev Posad), about 60 kilometres from Moscow, was always a must-see for official visitors from Canada.

The 16th century Church of the Ascension standing atop a high bank of the Moscow River at Kolomenskoe was featured in the 1990 movie The Russia House *based on the book by John Le Carré.*

In the early nineties Petrovsky Palace in Moscow housed an Air Force Academy. Many Soviet astronauts, including Yuri Gagarin, studied there. It was from the Petrovsky Palace that Napoleon began his hasty retreat from Russia in 1812.

14

Zhiguli, Zhukov, and Japanese Socks

"No wonder they call this place Ukraine," a foreigner remarked, surveying the yellow construction cranes on Kiev's skyline in the early nineties. Unfortunately all the signs of new building didn't mean the country was booming.

We made several trips to Ukraine. Once, in late October of 1992, we drove to Kiev from Moscow in our four-door Zhiguli via the cities of Tula and Oryol. It rained on the journey, and the roads became slippery and wet because they had been built without any sloping shoulders and drainage ditches.

Gasoline was in short supply. Besides leaving with a full tank from Moscow, we had eighty litres of petrol in containers in the trunk. In Kiev we would have to find more gas for the journey back. We had snacks and drinks for the 1,000-kilometre journey, because there were no roadside cafés en route to buy food. Except for the hotel restaurant at Oryol, where we stayed overnight and ate dinner and breakfast, inviting refreshment stops just didn't exist.

Industrial Tula is famous for making guns and the attractive brass samovars that many foreigners buy at Moscow museums or flea markets but find they have to leave behind at customs because they break an antiquities rule. At one time diplomats could smuggle old art, sculptures, and carpets out of the country under the noses of the authorities because their baggage was not searched; diplomats were no better than the ordinary foreigner who tried to remove the country's treasures, especially during the turmoil of 1991–92 when everything was for sale. But, by the time we left in the mid-nineties, a Ministry of Culture representative was on hand with nearly every diplomatic move to check that the documentation for *objets d'art* matched the items being shipped.

Near Tula, there was a large airborne division that figured prominently during a parliamentary uprising in Moscow in 1993, the following year. We didn't stop to take a look because a new west bypass took us away from the city.

The road from Tula to Kiev via Oryol is full of military history. The area was devastated during the German invasion of the Second World War and smashed again when the Red Army drove the intruders back. Just south of Oryol is Kursk where the biggest tank battle of the whole war was fought. It was a turning point for the Soviets, who then chased the Germans across Ukraine to the Polish border. Russia's greatest commander, Marshal Georgi Zhukov, was the military leader in charge.

Just south of Tula is Yasnaya Polyana, the estate of Count Leo Tolstoy. That's where we stopped to eat our sandwiches. We didn't have time to visit the museum, but we did use its primitive toilets. (Now one of Tolstoy's great grandsons has restored the estate to its former splendour.)

The next day we crossed into Ukraine without any border formalities. Two diplomats could never have travelled in a car so far from Moscow just a year or so before. Of course we'd registered our journey with our "friends"—the Russian military liaison office in Moscow—so they knew approximately where we were at all times. They worked in conjunction with Ukrainian military intelligence, who kept an eye on our travels in their country via the diplomatic plates on our vehicle. They were recorded and reported as we passed the numerous GAI (state automobile inspectorate) posts on the highway. If we took too long between checkpoints, military intelligence would assume we'd been up to no good (e.g., taking photographs or the wrong roads) or been accosted by bad guys. That was how it was supposed to work anyway. We could see the GAI officers looking at our plates with binoculars as we approached, but we were never stopped. I imagined them saying flatly, "Here come the two Canadians." In an odd way it was a secure feeling to know we were under someone's constant care.

The drive was a good way to observe what was happening to the people as their country struggled to change course. The fields were full of fertile black soil: this area of Ukraine had been the breadbasket of the Soviet Union. In village after village it seemed life had stood still. Geese, chickens, and cows wandered the roads. The village pump was in use. Families rode donkey and pony carts. Babushkas in bright kerchiefs guided small children along muddy paths from the road to the backyards of their one-storey wooden cottages or *izbas*.

While we were there, I combined spying with journalism and wrote several newspaper articles about the fallout from the 1986 Chernobyl nuclear reactor disaster and visited hospitals for children with leukemia and other cancers as well as an affected family in Kiev. These people were brave and stoic. An international project to help the children who had been affected was getting off the ground at that time and any little bit of publicity was welcomed. Money and hospital equipment was badly needed, and our paper was read by some influential foreigners in Moscow and around the world who might contribute.

The rest of the time in Kiev was spent on official walks with an Intourist guide and in meetings. Things were in great flux and possession of the dollar was everything. Kiev was not one of my favourite places. Perhaps it was the weather (we never seemed to visit in the summer) or just the stress of changing times, but

Ukrainians always seemed so glum. It took something special to make them smile.

When the time came to buy gas for the long trip home, we realized the stationary lineups at the pumps in Kiev were worse than in the country. We were so low on gas that Sam stopped at a GAI post and asked where would be the best place to go as we were heading for Russia. The officer looked at our plates and consulted with his chums. They agreed that we should try a gas station about sixteen kilometres out of the city on the road to Oryol.

We reached the station and were disappointed to see the pumps closed. A long queue of vehicles wound its way from the road and patiently encircled the small building. We drove in anyway and parked beside the pumps. No one honked at us or shouted. Everyone waited expectantly. The door of the pump house opened. A man came out. He looked at our plates. "Dollars," he said. We nodded. He filled us up and then filled our cans. He demanded an exorbitant price, but it couldn't be helped. We knew that gas was at a premium. Cars pulled in behind us. Surprisingly, the drivers winked and smiled at us. It didn't matter that we were served first; the pumps were working. They went on working too as we drove away. The GAI officer in Kiev had probably contacted the service station and would share in some of the profits. But at least we had gas.

Our most enjoyable trip to Ukraine took us by plane to Kiev and then by bus to Odessa and Sevastopol in 1993. We were joined for the bus ride by military attachés to Ukraine from Czechoslovakia, Hungary, and Poland, and by the Japanese naval attaché from Moscow. The object of the trip was to meet with the military commander of the Odessa district and explore some of his territory.

Since the Czechs, Hungarians, and Poles had only recently become friendly attachés, one had to exercise caution around them. On one hand the former Warsaw bloc countries were eager to be accepted as part of the western group: they would offer interesting tidbits that only they could know from their former association with Russia's military. On the other hand they still enjoyed many Cold War friendships and one didn't know if information was going both ways. But still, we were all supposed to be friends now. It was something that people in Ottawa, Washington, and London who had made spying their business for twenty or thirty years couldn't easily acknowledge.

Odessa, which is located on the Black Sea, is especially known for two famous exiles—Alexander Pushkin who lived there in the 1820s and Marshal Zhukov in the 1940s. Zhukov first made his name as a commander leading Russia's army in a victorious war against the Japanese in Mongolia in 1939. Then, after narrowly escaping Stalin's purge of the army officer corps, he battled for Moscow, Leningrad, Stalingrad, and Berlin in the Second World War and won them all. He had more important victories than any other Allied wartime commander. In 1945 Zhukov took the final surrender of the German Army in Berlin.

Zhukov's daughter, Ella, became a friend of mine in Moscow, and perhaps because of her stories about her father, Zhukov became one of my heroes. Ella and I travelled together to Zhukov's birthplace in the small village of Strelkovka outside of Moscow. His parents were poor: his father was a cobbler while his mother was a field worker. Zhukov and his sister also toiled in the fields when they weren't in school.

We visited his humble wooden home, now a museum. Strelkovka sits beside a wide river—a pastoral setting with yellow wheat fields and green meadows dotted with grazing black and white cows. But even the impressive statue of Zhukov, and the roads and laneways of small shuttered *izbas* painted in charming traditional blues, greens, and yellows couldn't hide the fact that economic circumstances were still dire.

At the age of twelve in 1908, Zhukov left the village to work in Moscow. He was apprenticed to his uncle, a furrier, and often badly treated and beaten. But he survived and, besides becoming adept at the fur trade, became an avid reader. When he was eighteen, Zhukov was called up to serve in the Tsar's army in the First World War. Three years and a revolution later, he joined the Red Army and climbed from the ranks to officer as he helped rout the White Army. In 1920 he married a young schoolteacher, and they had two children: Ira, born in 1928, and Ella, born in 1937.

Although a war hero, in 1946 Zhukov found himself at the mercy of a jealous Stalin and the head of the secret police, Lavrenti Beria. If Zhukov hadn't been so internationally well known (he had met and become friendly with Eisenhower and Montgomery in Berlin), he would probably have been executed or sent to a gulag. But instead the two chose to send him into obscurity—first to Odessa on the Black Sea and then to the Urals to command very secondary military districts.

Banished, Zhukov disappeared from world view. But after Stalin's death, Khrushchev restored Zhukov for a while to be his first deputy minister of defence. This enabled Zhukov to have his revenge on Beria—he signed his death warrant. But again Zhukov proved too popular with the people and, accused by Khrushchev of "Bonapartism" (the intention to seize power), he once again found himself pushed from the spotlight.

Zhukov's time in the Crimea has a Canadian connection. In 1954 the Soviet Army needed volunteers to test the impact of atomic bomb radiation fallout on military personnel. Odessa residents were invited to become guinea pigs and witness an atomic explosion at a remote site in Kazakhstan in return for shopping privileges at special military clothing and grocery stores. Among the volunteers was a young woman who would survive the horrifying experience by mere chance, and one day immigrate to Canada.

The story was told to me by Galina Petrova, a friend of our Russian language teacher, Oleg. She was a volunteer nurse at an Ottawa hospital on Christmas Eve in the early nineties, when one of her patients, an eighty-eight-year-old Russian-speaking woman, beckoned her over. Natalya Mischenko was very ill, but her mind was active and she had a story to tell before she died.

In the fifties, Natalya worked as a secretary at the headquarters of the Odessa Military District where Zhukov had been the commander. She and her friends had volunteered to watch the atom bomb test in Kazakhstan because they had been promised a shopping spree; it had been a long time since they had seen butter, coffee, and sugar. Volunteering with Natalya was a woman in her twenties called Larissa. She was a typical blond Russian beauty who wore her hair braided about her head. She and Zhukov were rumoured to be lovers, and of course Zhukov was going to be at the bomb testing site.

Ten women, including Natalya and Larissa, dug themselves into trenches about five kilometres from the blast site. The actual detonation was 400 metres above the ground's surface. Just before the final countdown, Natalya felt she should take medication to calm her down; her heart was beating fast with anticipation and excitement. She crept out of the trench and into the hut where the medicines were kept.

She didn't even bother to read the label on the bottle. It looked like the liquid tranquilizer she always used. She swallowed a few drops quickly. She was to find out almost immediately from the burning sensation in her throat that what she had taken was not a tranquilizer but iodine. Back in the trench, she watched the terrible sight of the mushroom cloud. Shortly afterwards she was taken to hospital.

She didn't see Larissa again for a year. The iodine had caused her so many problems—severe hyperthyroidism (elevating her heart and metabolic rates) and a raw swollen throat and thorax, both stripped of mucus—that she had spent months convalescing in Kazakhstan. When she did meet her friend on the street in Odessa in 1955, Larissa told her that out of the ten women in the trenches only she and Natalya remained alive. The other eight had all died from radiation poisoning. "It's only you and me now, Natalya," she remembers Larissa saying. Within a year Larissa was also dead. Only Natalya lived, and Soviet doctors told her that it was thanks to the iodine she drank. According to them, it had displaced the effects of radioactive iodine from the fallout on her thyroid gland, enabling her to escape the usually fatal result of radiation exposure. (After Chernobyl, some doctors fed seaweed, because of its high iodine content, to Ukrainian victims of radiation. But the conclusion was that iodine ingested after the fact didn't help much.)

Natalya saw her daughter grow up and immigrate to Canada with her husband, and later moved there to live with them. She wasn't afraid to die, she told the Ottawa nurse. After all, she did cheat death all those years ago.

I had this story in my head when the charming commander of the military district met us in Odessa and showed us the city. I couldn't help thinking of Zhukov in his stead. The commander posed with us for photographs on Odessa's famous 192 waterfront steps, immortalized in the classic 1925 film *Battleship Potemkin,* and invited us to dine with him the following night in Sevastopol, which had been a closed city just a short time before.

It was spring and the weather was warm. We and the other visiting military attachés were housed in a sanatorium near the beach. It had previously been a very exclusive retreat for senior military personnel. We walked down to the Black Sea even though I didn't even dare put my feet into the water, which was polluted from the indiscriminate dumping of waste and from the filthy stuff the various great rivers from Eastern Europe were emptying into the sea. But this didn't deter our Czech, Polish, and Hungarian compatriots who were used to pollution and made of sterner stuff. They were soon in the water and lying on the not very clean beach. They were also planning a trip to Odessa's famous mud baths. When I heard that the mud had an electrical current running through it to create that "extra tingle," I decided I'd forgo such a delight. I've always had a healthy respect for electricity.

The wives of the Eastern European contingent were just wives: no secret training for them. As a result, it was strictly forbidden to discuss anything serious in front of them, like "Let's hope we manage to get a good look at so and so…" in Sevastopol.

The harbour tour in Sevastopol was everything Sam and I had hoped for because it included a huge aircraft carrier that the Soviets had only recently completed before the fall of Communism. Now it sat idly awaiting its fate as talks were going on between Russia and Ukraine as to who would get what of the Black Sea Fleet. Our small boat toured past the hulking shape, and our attaché cameras, videos, and binoculars were out. Our Ukrainian military hosts couldn't help laughing at our enthusiasm. The job of attaché to the former Soviet Union was obviously losing a lot of its seriousness. A few months before, military intelligence in Ottawa would have died for photos like these. Now the Russian and Ukrainian navies didn't mind because they were hoping for a buyer. They were using us to provide them with free publicity. I think the aircraft carrier was eventually sold to India.

We were staying overnight in the naval city and dinner was in the officers' mess. The evening started normally enough. At the head of a long table sat our hosts, the senior Ukrainian brass. The food was plentiful and the drink, especially the vodka and local champagne, flowed. Before long, we could see that the Japanese naval attaché was getting quite intoxicated. Then it was time for some Slavic songs. I think years of drinking vodka improved the vocal chords in the Soviet Army. We went through all the usual medleys, Ukrainian folk songs mixing with Russian ones.

Then to our surprise the Japanese captain rose from his seat and moved slowly down the table until he was behind the Ukrainians. He started to mime the singers, conduct a non-existent orchestra, and even play an imaginary instrument or two. Confidently entertaining, our hosts were unaware of his presence. I couldn't imagine this happening in Zhukov's time. We would all have been terrified. He had an explosive temper.

But this commander carried on as if nothing was happening. The attachés watching were both horrified at the diplomatic blunder and in stitches from laughter. Neither of these two feelings could be registered on our faces. Only our bodies shook like jelly. It wasn't until the trembling hand of my Czech neighbour knocked over my glass of wine that the pressure was released. We could laughingly mop up the accident. In the confusion our Japanese friend then sidled around to us and whispered to Sam, "Look after me please," and then went and slumped in his seat.

A few minutes later, however, he came alive when the Ukrainians announced we all had to sing a song. Ironically they called on the Japanese attaché first. He jumped to his feet, stood to attention, and sang a perfect version of "The Japanese Sunflower Song." Then he sat back and put his head on his arms. We sang "The Maple Leaf Forever." Sam had learned it at school and could remember all the words. It also has a good tune and a rousing ending. French Canadians don't like it, but there was nothing political in us singing it. It has a good ring and the words don't matter to foreign ears.

Since our Japanese friend from Moscow had asked us to look after him, he became our responsibility. We helped him into the limousine that drove us to our floating hotel, a battleship moored in the harbour. Although a naval captain, he negotiated the steep gangway and swaying decks with difficulty. Then when we reached his cabin he seemed reluctant to stay inside. Fortunately it was close to ours so we could hear his ever-opening door. We decided not to go to bed until he was asleep. By that time the Ukrainians had caught on to the fact he was incapacitated and were curious. They had never before seen an inebriated Japanese naval captain.

He popped out of his cabin five or six times. Each time he was a little bit more undressed. Outside was always a reception committee. On his last trip into the passageway he had on just a pair of white boxer shorts and white socks. Everyone's attention was drawn to the socks—they were made with individual toes. Apparently this is a Japanese thing, but none of us had seen similar socks before. This was the cue for Sam to take the naval captain back to his cabin and make sure he stayed there until he fell asleep.

A few weeks later we were guests at a dinner at the naval captain's apartment in Moscow. I made a light-hearted comment during the evening about Japanese socks. His wife turned to me with a questioning look. I caught the face of the attaché over her shoulder and changed the subject.

15

Bugs and Bottles

I was very lucky that as a diplomat and a military attaché's wife I could go out to work in a normal way. It would have been impossible during the Cold War. An independent newspaper like the *Moscow Tribune* would not have existed, and I would have been hounded on the streets, in the subway, and at my destination by the KGB. Foreign diplomats could count on being followed.

Still, I knew several attachés wondered if it was too early for me to be out mingling with the masses in the local workplace. Wasn't there still an active security service just waiting to harass me or compromise me for giving lifts to Russian colleagues who were really KGB agents?

Perhaps the elderly man who worked for Pravda in Australia and now went through the Russian newspaper cutting out good story ideas for us was still active in the security police? Or perhaps it was our military correspondent, whose father was a colonel in the Russian Air Force. In fact, I doubt whether either of them had any interest left in spying. Now, they were all trying to make a living earning dollars.

Although I was aware the security services could be anywhere, I thought they might have given up on me now, pottering to work every day in my Lada, driving alongside the Moscow River. It was petty crime I was more concerned with. One unpleasant result of the new market economy was poverty: foreigners had become targets for petty theft. I tried to look as Russian as possible as I mingled with commuters. I could do nothing about my red diplomatic licence plates when I was on the streets.

The security police were definitely more concerned with Sam when we were in the city, and they checked him closely. Whether he left the building to meet another western attaché, to go to lunch, or to go shopping, someone fell in step behind him. Still, it was overt and non-threatening.

Sometimes their attentiveness was helpful, such as on our long drive home from Kiev to Moscow in 1992. We drove our Zhiguli through the day and half the next night without a hotel stop. The weather turned rotten during nightfall, and our windshield wipers ran out of fluid. We could hardly see. We were on a dark stretch of road not close to any village, but we spotted a light in front of a large shed. Fortunately we carried extra wiper fluid in the trunk and pulled in under the light to carry out what was supposed to be an easy operation.

Sam flicked a lever under the dashboard and got out. He walked to the front of the vehicle and tried to lift the hood. Nothing happened. He came back and tried the lever again. Again, nothing. If we couldn't add the fluid, driving would be dangerous. Suddenly, out of the shadows stepped two men. They must have been watching us. I don't know where they came from. I hadn't heard a car. They approached at an uncertain pace, like drunks. I was very apprehensive. They were close by now and watching Sam. He saw them and tried to lift the hood with even more urgency.

Then one of the men tapped him on the shoulder and pointed to the front of the car. The man stepped up close to the windshield and lifted the hood easily with one hand. Sam had been trying to raise it from the wrong end! Well, they didn't teach opening Zhiguli hoods at spy school. Gratefully, we offered the two men packages of American cigarettes that we always carried on us, but they only accepted one cigarette each. They weren't local Good Samaritans; they were minders.

Then there was the time Diane Mason was running for a Moscow subway train. At the last minute she tripped, and her foot plunged between the car and the platform. It might have meant a broken leg, but fortunately she didn't fall far. In an instant, two strong hands took hold of her arms, and she found herself being hoisted up and through the door onto the train. These helpers then melted away into the crowd, which left her in no doubt as to who they really were.

The KGB was active around the apartment. We accepted the fact that the maids we employed were still reporting on us. During those early years, though, their bosses must have been quitting the government at an alarming rate to go into business for themselves. They might be still reporting, but did the receivers care anymore? The enthusiasm for harassment must have been waning.

It was hard to tell sometimes what was or wasn't official harassment. Canadian attachés regularly came home from trips to find their car tires were flat and someone had propped open the door of their freezer refrigerators and ruined their food supply. Tires could easily be pumped, but in the early nineties, many foreigners were still ordering in food from a catalogue provided by a Danish company. Perishables like meat and dairy products from the few western stores that were open were very expensive. "How much for that ham? One hundred US dollars? I'll take two." We could live on the local economy if we really had to, but refrigeration was severely limited then, and we didn't want to poison our guests. The chopping blocks at local markets were not a pretty sight, containing years of dried blood.

There were lots of stories about apartments being entered, and we assumed telephones and other bits of the apartment were bugged. Ottawa had told us that if we wanted to discuss something important we were to take a walk. Even pillow talk was out. But this was advice given when we were undergoing training in Canada in 1991. Since then guidance coming from Ottawa was sparse.

We were aware that other western attachés were much more tightly controlled by their military intelligence handlers at home. "Go here, go there, take this photograph, talk to that person," they were directed. Whether by design or not, we were mostly left to our own devices as to where we should travel and to whom we should speak. Our knowledge didn't suffer much, we noticed, when we exchanged notes with the other foreign attachés in the secret, bug-proof, windowless rooms located in every foreign embassy.

Ottawa was now being inundated with information from spies and defectors. The information we sent in the diplomatic bag was important in substantiating some of their stories.

We discovered quite by accident that there was a piece of listening and maybe video equipment inside or near the living room television. We had cable TV that gave us CNN and BBC, although the picture wasn't clear. We also purchased a new videocassette and stereo system and wanted to hook everything up. So I squeezed behind the wall unit that housed the existing components to pull all the plugs from the wall. There was hardly any breathing space behind the cabinet, but there were certainly a lot of wires. Sam threaded new wires and plugs through to me, and I connected them as instructed. Despite our efforts, we couldn't get the television or video to work properly, and that evening we had to leave on a trip.

When we came back three days later the television set was working perfectly and so was everything else including the stereo. I know I hadn't plugged it in. It was obviously a job by our faithful listeners, who did not want us fiddling behind the wall unit and interfering with their equipment forever. They were probably more electronically minded than us.

Another unexplained event occurred when Sam was away on a three-day trip to Georgia with a vice-consul from the Canadian embassy. I had settled down to a quiet evening with Basil the cat and a book. It was Basil who heard the sound first. It was dripping water coming from the ceiling of the spare bedroom. No sooner had I finished fetching a bucket for the drips when I heard the same sound in the bathroom, then in the hall, the living room, the dining room, and the kitchen. It was coming down the light sockets, through the wall at the light switches, and from all the corners of the ceiling. What was going on?

Running out of bowls to catch the water, I went upstairs to the apartment above. There was no answer to my knock. There was nothing for it. I would have to get the drunken caretaker, who lived on the first floor, to open the door. He was shifty, untrustworthy, and unkempt in a drunk's way. He smelled of alcohol most of the time. He opened the door, and I explained the predicament. I needed to see my neighbour's apartment. I showed him my dripping walls and then locked my apartment door carefully. But not before he had spotted the storage cabinet containing liquor near the bathroom door. His eyes gleamed.

Then we went upstairs where he forced open the door. The apartment was under inches of water. The entrance hall sloped down into the living room so it was just sitting there, waiting to come down on me. Where was it coming from? We found out. The cistern was running continuously, and someone had wedged a brick firmly in the toilet. The owner of the apartment, a Turkish journalist, was away. With difficulty (he had to put one hand on the wall to steady himself), the caretaker removed the brick and fixed the cistern. The toilet gurgled happily back to normal.

Apparently the caretaker had a sort of vacuum that would suck up all the water. But for a price. He walked down the stairs behind me and stood in my doorway. I knew what he wanted. I wasn't going to give him the whisky he had spied, but I managed to make him go away with a bottle of vodka.

The Turkish journalist returned a few days later to a soggy floor.

He came down and apologized for any damage that might have been caused by the flood and said he was completely mystified by the appearance of the brick. It certainly hadn't been in his apartment when he'd left.

I was worried that now the caretaker had seen the stash of drink we kept for entertaining, he might be back with reinforcements. I was right. It wasn't that night but several weeks later. We were awakened by loud banging on the door. Just a few days earlier the embassy had installed a steel door on our apartment, replacing a wooden one decorated with a Canadian flag that had stood in the building for years. Personal security had become necessary in Moscow. Democracy was widening the gap between the haves and the have-nots. People were desperate to get their share of the new spoils. The less active surveillance of some foreigners by security police had not gone unnoticed by the criminal element.

The banging did not cease. In fact they were now trying to break down the door. We could see through the peephole there were three of them. We called the guards at the embassy, and they responded right away. They were not allowed to run around armed, but they could carry baseball bats with them. The hammering on the door went on. The handle was being manipulated with an instrument in some way when we heard the arrival of the first Canadian. The criminals scattered, but one was caught. He happened to be the caretaker's son.

Before we left Moscow the old man died. We smelled smoke in the hall one night. It was coming from the caretaker's room. He had fallen asleep in a drunken stupor, a burning cigarette in his hand. The firefighters told us to go back to our apartment. They had put out the blaze, and it was all over.

Bottles of alcohol were often used to placate people in those days. In fact, two brushes we had with the law were settled amicably by drink. Obtaining gas for vehicles was becoming a problem in Moscow. There was one twenty-four-hour station that was popular and did seem to have gas on Kutuzovsky Prospekt, opposite Victory Park. In the middle of the night Sam decided to drive down to the park and fill our two cars, his Zhiguli and my Lada Sputnik. All went well with the Zhiguli. Since there was no one on the roads, he made an illegal U-turn on the main street to head back to the apartment. He then did the same thing with the little red Lada.

Unfortunately, his illegal turn was seen by two patrolling traffic cops. They were after him in a flash and pulled him over. Both vehicles had red plates so they knew exactly what they were dealing with. After the initial study of his driving documents, they only had one question, "Did he have any whisky in the car?" No, Sam replied, but he did have some at home. "You lead the way, we'll follow," came the reply.

So my husband drove home and parked the car in its usual spot. The *militsia* followed him quietly and pulled in under the shadow of the building. Sam came upstairs and chose a bottle of whisky. He took it down to the two men, and they saluted him and drove off. This transaction was observed by the security men (KGB or similar) who guarded the apartment building and its parking lot. Since they were also hoping for their bottle at some future date, nothing would be said.

I also settled a little run-in with the police by means of a bottle. I left work one night at seven. It usually took me about twenty minutes to drive home. I had reached the traffic lights on the Moscow River embankment near the Radisson Slavanskaya Hotel. It was dark and snowing slightly. The traffic lights turned to green, and I started up. Then I realized that the car in front hadn't moved. Too late I slammed on the brakes, but my car skidded forward. The car in front was even smaller than mine, a little box on wheels from Ukraine. I knocked his bumper onto the road. My headlights crumbled and broke.

Unfortunately, the accident occurred right under the nose of a manned traffic police post. Dressed in their heavy sheepskin coats, they were already clambering down as the man in front was threatening me through the window and demanding dollars. If it had been away from the bright lights, I probably would have given him some dollars to replace his bumper. Insurance was unheard of. My car would be repaired by mechanics at the embassy so I wasn't worried about it. But now the police were involved.

The *militsia* shooed the other driver away as if he didn't matter. When he went away empty handed with his bumper in his trunk, I felt sorry for him. Then one of the burly officers got into the front passenger seat, and we started to verbally joust.

He wanted me to sign an accident form, and I didn't want to. I knew I wasn't supposed to sign anything. I was a diplomat, and that was one of the rules. "Call the embassy if you run into difficulty with the police," I remembered being told at a briefing. But call from where? Those were the days before everyone carried a cellphone. We sat for hours. Three I think. It was cold, and I wondered what I should do. I wasn't very far from home.

Finally I gave in. I tried my best to tell the officer about the road being slippery. He wrote something down, and I signed it. At that point I didn't care if I was signing that I had stolen the Kremlin jewels. I really wasn't worried about breaking diplomatic rule; I had done my best.

Then he said I couldn't possibly drive myself home because my headlights were broken. He would drive me home. I wasn't happy, but it was a *fait accompli*. He drove like it was the first time he had ever driven a car. We lurched along. He took a back route, past Kievskaya Railway Station and a market. I was a bit worried at first, but he soon turned back towards Bolshaya Dorogomilovskaya Street and crossed into our parking lot. It was at that moment I realized why he was driving me home, followed by a friend in a police car. After all, driving such a short distance without lights wasn't particularly dangerous; in Russia cars drove using dim sidelights most of the time.

Sam was just leaving the parking lot to search for me. He glanced at the policeman who was driving and followed my Lada over to the shadowy spot we knew the GAU liked. I said to Sam, "Could you go upstairs and get a bottle?" He knew what to do. Whisky in hand, the officer made a big ceremony of tearing up my "report."

16

Kravchenko

The collapse of the Soviet Union followed by market reform was almost unbearable for most Russians: it was like the aftermath of a war. Desperate for money, pensioners sold the contents of their homes on the sidewalk while others were reduced to going through garbage bins. A nation of animal lovers suddenly let their dogs loose on the streets because they couldn't afford to feed them. People who had once had a job and a guaranteed paid annual holiday under Communism were now without a pay cheque, whether they had work or not.

It devastated all strata of society, except the opportunists and political insiders who eventually became the New Russian elite. It certainly affected artists, writers, and the intelligentsia. Some of the country's best painters and sculptors, whose work was displayed in the nation's museums, began selling off their art. The Soviet Artists' Union had folded, government perks had dried up, and artists needed the cash.

We became art collectors. Who could resist? The art was good, and the prices at the beginning of the nineties were rock bottom. The House of Artists near Gorky Park had already become one of our favourite Sunday haunts. It was always busy because it was a place for young Muscovites to meet outside their parents' cramped apartments. They wandered the halls looking at the paintings and sat holding hands in the buffet over cups of tea. The exhibitions began to change more and more often. Most of the paintings were for sale, and all the prices were negotiable. Then the first private galleries started to spring up, and it was in one of these that we found our first Grigori Kravchenko.

It was a large painting of a boy listening to his grandfather spinning tales in an old stable. The artist had captured the Russian face of the old man, his flat cap, the special way he held his glowing-tipped cigarette, and the faithful bottle of cognac by his side. The boy was wearing his grandfather's old army cap as he listened enthralled. The cap, cocked to one side, displayed a red star.

At first the gallery owners told us it wasn't for sale because the painting was "museum-quality." We agreed with them, but badgered them into selling. It was a time when everything and anything in Russia had a price, and what we offered was enough to enable the owners to buy other works, pay some bills, and stay in business. They took the money. When we got the painting home, we knew we had to meet the artist.

His hometown of Krasnodar was more than 1,000 kilometres from Moscow. Fortunately for us it was located in a strategic area in southern Russia near the new Muslim administrative district of Adygeya.

We set up interviews with the mayors of Krasnodar and Adygeya and officially arranged to visit artist Kravchenko in his studio. If we had planned the meeting privately, either we or Kravchenko would have been in trouble. We were allowed to go to the studio on our own, but we had followers throughout our stay. We hoped they liked art. Kravchenko's studio was located behind some colourful, mostly pale blue *izbas* in an old area of the city. We had to walk through neglected back gardens, children's play areas, and past a row of outdoor toilets belonging to the houses. There were four toilets, all in need of repair and paint, but with the usual wooden seat and round hole. Two were occupied by elderly men who'd been sitting, enjoying a chat, with the doors open. They nonchalantly watched our approach, their newspapers for reading and cleaning in hand.

We finally found Kravchenko. He appeared small because he was slightly stooped, but his wild grey hair crammed beneath a dark blue beret, his beard, and his blue-grey eyes gave him a fierce look. He was about sixty years old, a professor at the local art school, and he wore an artist's smock that matched the colour of his beret.

In his small, shed-like studio, the floors and walls were strewn with oil paintings, so many you couldn't avoid walking on them. Then he started to pull out more and more canvases from shelves. It was a gold mine, a promised land of art. The paintings, dating from the sixties, depicted family, neighbours, factory workers, and scenery from the Urals to southern Russia. Even the users of the outside toilets with their open-door policy had been captured in oils. We understood from what he said that in the seventies he had fallen out with officialdom because of his art. Consequently, his name was on the black list, meaning he hadn't been able to sell his works. But he had gone on painting just the same.

Some of the paintings were still not for sale by order of his daughter Oksana. These were of the immediate family. But we did manage to buy a striking self-portrait of the artist and a painting of his wife. They were Rembrandt in style. We also bought some social realist paintings of factory workers. The workers weren't happy and laughing, the way they were in the usual government-approved art. These workers leapt at you from the canvas with eyes both glowering and glowing. We bought five, the most we could carry onto the plane.

We walked happily back to the hotel, but when we got there, we found that the self-portrait hadn't been signed. There was no way of contacting Kravchenko other than rushing back to his studio and hoping he was there. He was and willingly walked back to the hotel, clutching some paintbrushes to sign his work. He stood in front of the canvas for a moment and then wrote "Grigori Kravchenko 1980." Then he rubbed out the date with his thumb and wrote "77" instead. At least it was a smudge by the artist himself. He looked around our hotel room before he left, saying, "I wondered what it was like in this hotel. It is only for rich people." We were embarrassed. To us, the hotel was nothing special. Had he asked enough for his paintings? He had obviously lived a very frugal life.

We visited the city's art galleries and museums with the secret police hard on our tail. Not art lovers after all, they left us to browse inside and then rejoined us outdoors. When we reached the end of the city's main street, we decided to catch a bus back to our hotel. We waited, and they waited. Finally a bus came, but it was jam-packed. We jumped on and then finding it too suffocating, jumped off. The bus pulled away with several minders looking at us through windows at the rear. They were not amused.

The second morning in town my husband went out early to get some fresh air. Leaving the hotel, he had the usual feeling of being observed. He saw a woman standing as if she were waiting for someone on the sidewalk, but she was among a crowd and paid no attention to Sam as he passed. He walked down the street and then turned left towards a market. He stopped by some stalls selling "fur" hats. Only the hats closely resembled the hair of the numerous wild dogs around town. Then he watched a man who was holding a live pig while trying to open the trunk of his car. He had a rope tied around the pig's leg, and each time he got the key in the lock, the animal would jerk frantically and pull the man away from the vehicle. The pig was desperate to escape the dark confines of the trunk. While he was watching this fight between man and beast, Sam heard the sound of running footsteps. He was shielded from the sidewalk by a truck parked in the road. Suddenly the woman from outside the hotel went running by. She had mislaid her quarry and would be in trouble with her bosses.

In the late afternoon we visited Adygeya to meet the mayor in the capital city Maykor. The friendly assistant to the mayor of Krasnodar accompanied us, and his driver drove us to the Muslim enclave skirting the Kuban Sea, a huge reservoir created in the seventies. We were told that the water table had risen so high that more than 3,000 square kilometres of farmland and thousands of homes were flooded.

Our car stopped in Maykor and waited for a second black Volga to join us. Our destination was a country club on the outskirts of the city. It had been another KGB dacha for visiting Communists in the Soviet era while now the same security service ran it as a hunting lodge for local officials and their guests.

There were several men at the country club waiting for our entourage. Two mayors, their assistants, Sam and I, and about ten additional guests sat down to a vast spread. Others stayed lurking in the background. First came numerous salads and cold cuts, sliced fish and caviar, the usual Russian *zakuski*. After these dishes came hot chicken, lamb, and potatoes. Dessert was locally baked cake with cream and nuts. Of course there was plenty of alcohol, mostly local cognac and vodka, and a few soft drinks like Pepsi and Fanta.

We began to understand why there were so many present: it was curiosity. It was the first time any of them, all members of internal security in some way (even the mayors), had ever entertained a foreign military attaché. Yeltsin's new "democracy" was creating some unusual encounters: yesterday's Cold War foes were becoming today's dinner partners, even though several in the room had followed us around the city earlier. Numerous toasts were made. The mayor of Adygeya assured us that just because his new enclave was Muslim didn't mean it would create trouble. It would stay in Russia. End of discussion on that subject. I stopped taking notes. Our hosts then turned the session into one of mutual admiration. We were both huge countries, we shared the same seas, the same landscape, similar weather, vast mineral resources, fought on the same winning side in the Great Patriotic War ... They seemed to be genuinely enjoying our company; it wasn't the usual ploy of seeing just how drunk they could make a pair of foreign spies. Our job was still to report on them, and their job was to report on us, but the new touch was the human contact without fear of repercussions.

Even after four hours, the dinner was not quite over. The last toast was outside. Ten cognacs on a tray had been carefully placed on the trunk of our car. They were all downed in one fell swoop except for mine. I was allowed to sip. Sam was overcome with an allergic reaction and started to sneeze. Fifteen times he gave a loud guffawing sound, and in an adjacent field about a dozen turkeys in a pen joined in the chorus in a loud gobbling approval. If our friends had laughed before, they were now hysterical. Tears streamed down their faces as they propped themselves against the cars and wall. Sam was a hit.

We reached the hotel room, and Sam quickly fell into a deep sleep. Our plane was leaving at 5 A.M. for Moscow, which meant we had a car arranged to pick us up at the hotel at 3:30. I was left with the packing—five large paintings and our bags. I went and asked the *dezhurnaya* (the woman who guards the floor) if she would sell me a few of the hotel's bed sheets. The sheets were sewn together like a duvet cover with a large hole in one side where a blanket could be tucked in to make a cozy comforter. The double sheets could also easily accommodate one or two paintings. We made a deal.

We saw Kravchenko again on another visit to Krasnodar. His studio had been discovered by Moscow entrepreneurs and cleaned out. We heard that his paintings were on sale for thousands of dollars in Moscow and the United States. I wonder how much of the money Grigori ever saw. Later, we met another artist, a student of Kravchenko's, and drank cognac, ate chocolate, and bought some paintings at his studio. We held a small reception for him in our Moscow apartment to introduce him to other Canadians, Americans, and Brits who had also become art lovers.

17

Chechnya

In 1993 we went to Grozny, the capital of Chechnya. At that time the country was in the throes of breaking away from Russia, and a former general in the Soviet Air Force, Dzhokhar Dudayev, had already declared he was president of the new republic.

We caught an Aeroflot flight to Grozny along with a British air force couple, Sean and Anne Reynolds, having made arrangements through the usual Russian military liaison office in Moscow. Reynolds was a bright, genuine, optimistic person, and he and Sam became good friends. Both were patient listeners and level-headed: important attaché attributes. Because we had only hand luggage when we landed at the airport, we went through the usual formalities quickly. We had appointments with various military and civilian dignitaries and assumed we would be met by a vehicle from one department or another. But there was no driver and no car. There were taxis, however, so we picked the nearest one and got in. We gave the driver the name of our Intourist hotel, and he set off.

Grozny resembled a normal Soviet city: lots of tall, dour grey concrete apartment buildings with stores hugging the sidewalks beneath, monolithic government buildings, a few hotels, a main square, and outdoor markets. There seemed to be more men on the streets than women, but people were dressed in well-worn but clean clothes, similar to those in far-away Russia. The only difference was the predominant grey astrakhan fur hats among the men. Life wasn't easy in the spring of 1993, it seemed, but it was endurable. Unbeknown to the residents then, they were about to face two wars in which their city would become a ghost town of bombed-out buildings where only the hopeless, helpless, and lawless would remain. Today, many are still living in refugee camps outside of Chechnya while the rebels continue to exchange fire and rhetoric with the Russian Army.

We were absorbed in looking at the city, and it was only when we entered the main square that we noticed that the driver had driven straight past the large Intourist hotel on our left. We told him to stop, but he kept on going. He had a mission and only he knew what it was. We then saw the tanks and armoured personnel carriers parked across the square and realized the taxi was heading straight for the group of armed Chechens gathered around them.

The men and heavy armoury were guarding a very large government building. There were dozens of men milling about carrying Kalashnikov rifles and dressed in black leather jackets and coats. The driver got out immediately when we stopped. He was shaking hands with the men and hugging them in the enthusiastic way men greet each other in that part of the world. He was nervous but making sure they knew he was on their side.

The men surrounded the taxi and opened the doors. The guns were pointed at us, and they gestured for us to get out of the car. This was no training exercise.

The four of us were herded into the entrance hall of the government building, which was packed with similarly dressed men carrying the same sorts of weapons. Everyone was very curious to see us arrive, and they crowded around the men who had "arrested" us. They seemed pleased with their captives, but a little uncertain what to do with us now.

After a few minutes someone senior arrived to talk to us. None of the guns were lowered while he did so. He was wearing a long black leather coat and had a broken nose. He explained our situation to us in Russian. Now that Chechnya had declared itself a republic and had its own president, all applications for travel through the area by foreigners had to go through the new administration, not through Russian channels. Therefore we were in Chechnya illegally.

We asked to be "taken to their leader." There was some discussion among the group, and then they chose one person, Sean Reynolds, to accompany them upstairs. He got into the elevator with several men.

Half an hour passed, and Sam was worried. He explained to the men surrounding us that he must find his colleague. They seemed quite happy to take him to the same elevator. That left just Anne and me entertaining the group in the lobby. One of the men had taken a liking to my jacket. "How much did that jacket cost?" The Chechen wanted to know. I told him about $100. That seemed like a lot of money to him. (How times have changed. My jacket would now be "too cheap" to wear.) The Kalashnikov-wielding Chechen fingered the material. I knew I would give it to him if the situation got any trickier.

The Chechens were getting bolder. They asked me about Canada, and I said it looked a bit like Chechnya. One of the men produced a silver coin and indicated that he wanted me to take it as a memento of my visit to Grozny. It was an old silver rouble bearing Tsar Nicholas' head. I took the coin because it was offered in such a way that I didn't want to offend him by refusing it; there are cultural differences in politeness. I noticed there was a hole in the coin, right through the Tsar's temple! I remained impassive as I pocketed it. I didn't want the Chechen to think I was fazed by the discovery. I was inclined to think it was a present rather than a message. Looking back on the atrocities committed soon afterwards in Grozny, I realize I was naive.

About forty-five minutes later our husbands returned, smiling, and it was obvious we were free to go. Whatever had happened upstairs was good news. The doors were opened for us, and we stepped out into the square. It was only a short walk across to the hotel, but we were aware of the curious eyes watching us, the guns and the armoured personnel carriers pointed in our direction. We walked nonchalantly carrying our bags. We didn't talk about the encounter and were careful not to smile.

There was just one woman at the hotel desk. She gave us the keys to our rooms. We were all on the same floor with just one room separating us. Since we were starving, we agreed to meet in the hotel restaurant in ten minutes.

As it turned out, there really was nothing to eat in Grozny's major hotel, except for greasy vegetable soup and dark bread, an indication of the region's dire economy. There was Miller beer, though, and each of us drank a bottle as we picked our way through the grease. The hotel had seen better times. As I walked to the table my foot sank into a damp hole underneath the carpet. It was the kind of place where one looked carefully under each slice of bread. At least we were able to talk in the restaurant. There was no one else in there, and no one around. Not even staff. Since we were able to sit at any one of a dozen tables, there was no chance of being recorded.

Sean told us he had been taken to the fourth-floor office of the minister of foreign affairs of the breakaway republic. The man spoke English and was amused to find a military attaché from a western country sitting in his office. There were guards everywhere, sitting in his outer office and lining the corridors. The minister explained that they were expecting Russia to react militarily (which it did) and had to be ready for anything. The fact he had a chance to explain all this to a foreign attaché, a spy, was to him a bit of a coup.

Sam had been ushered into the elevator and left there alone. Without a clue about where to go, he just guessed and pressed the button for the fourth floor. There he held the lift doors open and looked down the corridor. A lot of men were gathered outside of an office so he went down to investigate. Then the minister was entertaining two military attachés.

From all accounts, the minister did not fit the picture of the armed, Russian-hating, Bin Laden-trained religious fanatics that subsequently appeared in Chechnya. The men who initiated the breakaway mostly died in the first war that began at the end of 1994 and lasted a couple of years. They had some noble mission in mind to put the record straight for Chechen Muslims, who had been dealt a few rough hands, including deportation, during Stalin's time. Maybe they figured Chechnya could survive alone economically because the country was sitting on oil, and oil pipelines ran across it. But these first battles only served to create a hard-core bunch of revenge-seekers who earned money from kidnapping, stealing oil, and other crimes, and who in 1998 finally tested Russia's patience. We would not have walked away so easily from an encounter with that lot.

The Russian army has a lot to learn about winning the hearts and minds of people as they go about their business. A bit of good PR, like feeding, clothing, and educating the war refugees and rebuilding the cities and towns would ease some tension. But in Russia, appeasing Chechens would not win many votes for the government in places like eastern Siberia, where living conditions are abysmal, and heating, food, and jobs are in the same short supply.

The result of the interview with the foreign minister (who ten years later was still around and quoted in newspapers) was that the two men had been invited to meet with the new president of Chechnya the next morning at nine at his palace.

The soup did not sustain us for long. Fortunately we had with us the usual supplies, including a tin of corned beef. We walked about the city looking for something to go with it, and finally found some tomatoes for sale. Tomatoes are something Russia's southern regions and Central Asia do really well. Dark red, ripened but firm, they really smell like tomatoes. Not like the tasteless variety we endure in Canada. They have to be washed really well, and I hope the iodine treatment that removed the human manure, tainted soil, and animal contact won't affect us in the long run. We found white bread too. It was similar to the fresh, small white loaves baked by the state and delivered to Moscow's corner stores, only these had been baked on the premises.

Intourist hotel rooms nearly always came with glass-fronted cabinets containing cups, saucers, plates, and cutlery, as if they were expecting guests to eat in their rooms. Unfortunately food leftovers attracted cockroaches into the bedrooms. We ate and planned the strategy for the next day.

In the morning, Anne and I watched from a window as the two attachés walked across to the presidential palace. I had a video camera and was planning to go out onto the balcony to film their journey. It was a good story and the journalist in me didn't want to miss the start, even though the film was intended for Ottawa's eyes only.

I had them in my sights and was enjoying the warm sunshine when all of a sudden the armoured personnel carriers and gun-wielding security mob came into my viewfinder. Was it my imagination or were all their weapons pointing at me? I realized that from across the square, it might be hard to distinguish whether the sunlight was reflecting on a camera lens or the barrel of a weapon. I put the video camera down and went inside to wait. Even western troops in wartime have killed press cameramen when they mistook the cameras they were shouldering for missile launchers.

All three men at the meeting were air force officers. There's camaraderie among members of the military when they meet in a setting other than a warring one, even if they are not on similar ideological sides. They can chat in the language of "there I was upside down and nothing on the clock." President Dudayev, a bomber pilot, explained the reasons why Chechnya had decided to separate from Russia: the raw deals, the discrimination, the unsolved poverty that the Chechens had undergone and were still undergoing. "We can do better alone," he told them. A slight, moustached man, he had reached the rank of general in the Soviet forces and was courteous and precise to the two westerners. He died in the first of the two wars that followed.

There was only one tense moment. Since life was normal on the streets at that time, a wedding was in progress, and the decorated, horn-blowing cars were proceeding around the square. In Chechnya as in most of the Caucasus the celebrating also includes firing guns into the air from the windows of the vehicles. When the sound of gunshots reverberated in that ninth-floor office, Dudayev visibly flinched. His guards were immediately at the windows. The interview ended shortly afterwards.

We decided not to stay in Grozny. Through the hotel we managed to hire a taxi that would take us to Vladikavkaz, in North Ossetia.

Early the next morning our car arrived. We told the driver where we wanted to go, although the hotel would have told him already. He said very little, but before he started on his three-to-four-hour journey, he decided to take us on a tour of the city. Perhaps the people who were joining us for the trip weren't ready yet.

Sam sat in the front passenger seat with the video camera. I sat in the back with Sean and Anne. The driver freaked a little when he saw the camera, but gradually got used to it. He even liked it when the camera was panned across his side of the car.

There were other cars on the two-lane road but we knew instantly when the rest of our official followers were with us. They weren't shy about telling us. A car passed us with three young Chechens in it. They were younger than our driver who was ethnic Russian. If he was still working for some sort of security services, taking orders from Chechens would have been new to him. But everyone had to try and make ends meet somehow. He cheered up considerably when he saw the others go by. They looked into our car and grinned and waved, as if to say, "We know who you are."

They pulled in several cars ahead of us. Our driver immediately began to speed up. He became inspired and passed the car in front and then the one ahead of that. The road wasn't very wide, and the oncoming traffic squeezed to the right. He mentioned that he had never driven the route before, which didn't inspire confidence. The car was an old Volga, with no seatbelts in the back, and the seatbelts in the front hung broken and useless. We were going through some hilly countryside, dotted with oilrigs, and the road became curvy. Still, the terrain did not stop the two vehicles from engaging in a game of tag, chasing each other for about two hours.

Sometimes there were three cars passing each other all at the same time. We complained, but the driver ignored us. If he had put us out on the road, we would have had to pay a very large sum to get someone to pick us up.

At least the landscape started to get interesting. There were tanks and armoured personnel carriers parked along side roads. We assumed we were approaching the Chechnya-Ingushetia border. We were so thankful that the journey was almost over that we didn't see what lay on the road ahead. Neither did the driver. He was still concentrating on his friends who were behind us. At seventy kilometres per hour we hit a series of speed bumps. Our heads hit the roof, the driver slammed on the brakes. The chassis shuddered and seemed ready to detach itself from the body. Every bit of dust that had gathered in the car for the past twenty years came loose. We were choking and unable to see. The vehicle did a ninety-degree turn, slid sideways, and hopscotched over the final speed bumps. At last it stopped, and we all got out. Vehicles pulled around us, but there was no sign of the official party.

The driver was beside himself, but we didn't feel too sorry for him. We might have all been killed. As it was we were unhurt, but it was almost half an hour before the driver had the courage to put his car back on the road. We travelled more slowly the rest of the way.

The area we were entering of mainly Muslim Ingush and mostly Orthodox Christian Ossetians had seethed with national and racial hostilities for years. The conflict dated back to the 1944 decision by Stalin to deport the Ingush and the Chechens to the steppes of Kazakhstan for alleged collaboration with the Nazis during the Second World War. When the Ingush were permitted to return in 1957, they found Ossetians occupying their homes. In 1992, a brief war was fought over land in North Ossetia that both groups claimed. The outcome was the death of hundreds and the expulsion of some 75,000 ethnic Ingush. The two groups are still not reconciled, and the threat of war remains. Hatreds were inflamed in 2004 when the Beslan school hostage tragedy took place in North Ossetia killing more than 150 children.

That the 1992 conflict was not resolved was evident from the several roadblocks we passed as we crossed the region patrolled by Russian army troops with armoured personnel carriers and tanks. Then, in and around Vladikavkaz, the capital of North Ossetia, we saw burned-out buildings. Breaking his glum silence, the driver told us that they had been the homes of the driven-away Ingush.

We stayed at the Intourist hotel in Vladikavkaz. The bathroom wasn't bad if one ignored the slimy floor of the shower with the small piles of dandruff, which had assembled in the corners over the years, and the stained toilet *sans* lid. We showered off the road dirt and dried ourselves with thin terry hand towels and pressed white linen bath cloths.

The following day during a walk downtown, the Brits demonstrated just how overt they could be in collecting information. The first incident occurred as we were crossing a road behind a vehicle. A man approached us with a package. He was in his thirties and wore old blue jeans with a dark blue windproof jacket. We had been taught from day one of our training never to accept anything from strangers in the street, but Sean stopped, chatted to the man, and took the brown envelope. "He wants to go to the UK" was his explanation. Further down the road, outside some shops, another Georgian-looking fellow stopped Sean after quite obviously singling him out. I had walked a few paces ahead, and I turned around in time to see a man across the road taking a photograph of the meeting with a palm-sized camera. It was all over very quickly. The picture would be placed on file and only used when a few spies needed to be expelled for political reasons, or our fellow attaché fell into some warmer water. Who knew if either of the meetings were chance or had been planned? We weren't asking. Sean and Anne Reynolds weren't telling.

Around lunchtime we hired a car at the hotel to explore the beautiful Caucasus mountain countryside just outside the city. A drive along the Georgian Military Highway that passed close by was "*nelzya*" (forbidden), but our driver was happy to take us up through the winding mountain roads not far from the capital. We came to a mountain slope that he said was an ancient burial ground known as the "village of the dead." We drove for a while up the hill and then walked until we reached a cluster of about fifty stone beehive-shaped structures. Looking in openings in the stonework, we could see human skeletons lying on stone shelves in the tombs. The cold winds blowing through the buildings kept the old bones preserved and made us shiver. If we'd been movie-spies instead of real-life ones, the timing would have been perfect for a James Bond-type villain like Oddjob or Jaws to make a dramatic appearance.

The area was popular as a movie setting. In September 2002 a Russian film crew was working there when a 150-metre-high glacier broke off from the peak of a mountain and slid 25 kilometres to the highway leading to Vladikavkaz. The resulting avalanche—metres of ice and snow—buried the film crew and killed about 100 people, including a famous Russian movie actor.

As we drove away from the historic site, a white Zhiguli car came out of a side road and tucked in behind us. We passed through several villages before our driver asked if we were hungry. There was no sign that said "restaurant," but our driver pulled into the courtyard of a house just off the road. He went inside and was soon approaching us with what looked like a whole family—father, mother, and daughter. It was a café, said the driver, a place to stop for a good bowl of soup and fresh bread.

The head of the household, Vladimir, chatted as his wife and daughter served us hot vegetable soup with large pieces of floating meat, fresh homemade bread, and tea. A wood fire in the room made us feel warm, welcome, and comfortable. At the end of the meal we asked for our bill, and Vladimir, to our embarrassment, declared that he would accept no payment. We had become "his friends." Being a fair-minded Canadian, Sam decided to offer the man his Swiss army knife as a token of thanks. The reaction was startling. We hadn't realized how men in the Caucasus region would react to being offered a knife. It was a serious "I want to be your blood brother" sort of thing. (No doubt a knife proffered with the blade out and the handle pointing the wrong way might be greeted differently.)

"Now I have to give you something in return," said Vladimir. He went next door and returned with the polished brass casing from a small ammunition shell, about six inches high and two inches in diameter. He explained that the casing, now in use as a pencil and pen holder in Sam's study, had been a gift from his shipmates aboard the Soviet Navy vessel *Sevastopol* on which he had served for three years from 1971. It was engraved with the ship's name. He wanted my husband to have it. It would have been offensive to say, "No, I couldn't possibly." That sort of politeness is not well known in Russia. Once more we were in his debt. Then we remembered that as we had entered Vladimir's home we had seen a few small souvenirs for sale in the hallway. We each chose one of the wooden carved figurines, paid a few roubles for each, and felt a little better.

We rejoined our Intourist car for the drive back to Vladikavkaz, and the patiently waiting white Zhiguli fell in behind us.

18
Free Press and Ethics

From its beginning with less than a dozen employees, the *Moscow Tribune* had added four times the number of staff by the autumn of 1993. I started out as the only editor of the newspaper's stories, but gradually we added three more as well as reporters, designers, and advertising staff.

The *Tribune's* office was in an apartment in a block of flats on Leninsky Prospekt that had for years housed diplomats, including military attachés, and foreign journalists. Like our apartment building, it was run by the Soviet-era diplomatic corps administration bureau, *Glav.U.P.D.K.*, which oversaw all the housing for foreigners in Moscow during the Cold War and through whom we hired our maids. (When our son Charles married Miranda in 1994, we discovered that his wife's grandfather had lived at 45 Leninsky Prospekt in the early sixties when he had been the Canadian naval attaché to Moscow. Our grandchildren have spies on both sides of the family!)

The paper started in one apartment that had for years belonged to the publisher, Anthony, and his mother and father, Victor and Jennifer Louis. Then it expanded to another apartment across the hall. It was still cramped. At one point three typists, three editors, a news editor, a production manager, about ten reporters (American, British, Canadian, and Russian), and four designers were all crammed into three rooms and a kitchen. We shared one toilet and a bathtub (in which expats whose hot water had been cut off or who had been thrown out of their apartments often showered). The toilet shortage was relieved by two more across the hall where Anthony was located with his office manager, display advertising staff, accountants, and distribution drivers. There they also dealt with the walk-in classified advertisements for accommodation, jobs, visas, introductions, marriage, and massage. The latter ads could be racy and were loathed by the young, politically correct Americans working as reporters, but these classifieds contributed towards keeping the paper viable and paid wages.

Eventually as the paper grew, we spread out over four different apartments on two floors to house the additional editors, journalists, designers, news typists, and other production people. We stored the newspapers in the basement rooms that had until recently housed the KGB listeners and listening equipment that had been the bane of the building's occupants.

The office manager, Lena Kulyabina, eventually immigrated to Canada with her husband and two sons. It was from her that I learned about the poor conditions in ordinary Russian hospitals, and we did several stories on the subject. I had happened to mention that when I'd woken up that morning, I had found a cockroach sitting on my finger, looking at me. She laughed and said her mother had once woken up to find a pigeon sitting on her chest. Then she grew serious and said that hospitals were the place to find cockroaches.

Her son had gone into hospital for a leg operation. He complained that the cockroaches were climbing onto the bed and walking across the sheets and across his face. A boy in the next bed had been given a box of chocolates. In the morning the box was black with cockroaches. To combat the problem, Lena had taken a piece of chalklike poison from China (every Muscovite, including our maid, knew about this invaluable tool) and drawn a line around his bed so that the cockroaches stayed away. Unfortunately she couldn't do anything about the ceiling, and they continued dropping on her son from overhead.

Anthony did not have much luck with his advertising managers: not all of them were honest, and they often skimmed money for themselves. It cost the *Moscow Tribune* a lot. Since the newspaper lived from week to week, month to month on advertising revenue, getting paid on time and the right amount was a problem. Fortunately for us, there was a stream of new services opening, including hotels, restaurants, bars, nightclubs, groceries, and department stores that needed to advertise their existence. The paper was delivered free to them as well as to embassies for distribution among expats and English-speaking Russians. Selling the paper for roubles or even hard currency on the street was out of the question because of the logistics of collecting the money in chaotic new Russia. Overseas subscriptions were sold.

Adding to all the comings and goings of the resident staff were the contributors, freelancers, and correspondents who came in several times a week to bring in their columns and photographs. On Saturdays we had a large opinion page complete with editorials. The opinion was usually contributed, and we had no problem filling the space. The $100 US we offered for 1,000 words was considered good pay in Russia in the early nineties, and there were quite a few people in high places who liked to collect this fee. We didn't care about the writer's ideology as long as he or she had something interesting to say about current politics, the military, or the security services.

We had two foreign columnists who had worked as journalists in Russia for years and added to the paper's credibility. One was an American, Albert Axell, whose favourite expression was, "A little known fact about this is …" Then he went on to describe the "little known fact" that only he had somehow, somewhere, managed to unearth.

The other was an Australian, John Helmer. His contacts were good and his skill was in writing about scandals involving oligarchs, politicians, and current industrial development. He also knew everything there was to know about Russia's diamond industry. Like the American columnist, he kept detailed and reliable files. He was tall (as big as the office doorposts I always noticed) and thin and had long straggly grey hair. He usually wore a diplomat's typical long, navy blue woollen overcoat. His beat was the parliament, and I really enjoyed talking to him because he had inside information on what was going on in Russian politics and lots of other things besides.

Another interesting staff member was a talented Russian, Valeriy Mikhailov, who had worked for Radio Moscow (now called Voice of Russia) as an editor. He told me he had been one of the broadcasters who scheduled the music for those secret messages relayed to spies abroad—especially London—as portrayed in many movies and in spy novels. If it was Beethoven on Radio Moscow at midnight, then the spy could proceed with his clandestine business. If the spy heard Mozart, then he should hold off for a while. Was he pulling my leg? Like most intelligent Russians getting to know westerners better, he thought we were really a naive, uncultured lot.

I spent most of my time rewriting the contributions from Russians, either from the reporters we employed or the columnists. Copy from the columnists was usually poorly translated and often sounded like gobbledegook when I first embarked on it. But getting to the nub of the story was an achievement, like finishing a good crossword puzzle. The contributed news stories were minefields. I ended up with a story that read well, but were the facts correct? I double-checked them with the freelancers, but usually they just nodded in agreement with my finished draft, unwilling I suspected to point out misinterpretations in case it held up payment. "Publish and be damned" took on a whole new meaning.

Russians write news stories differently from us. At least they did then. The basic pyramid approach with the five Ws somewhere near the first paragraph just didn't apply. The story's main thrust was always hidden somewhere in the bowels of the piece. The first part was all chatty nonsense, then the story would jump out, and then it would peter off into more speculation. Add to this a bad translation, and you could see what faced the editors every day. I think it had something to do with the skill of hiding the facts during the years of Communism.

This problem was compounded when freedom of the press entered the picture. Many local journalists immediately switched from the suppressed *Pravda* style of writing to *Frank* without knowing that the norm was *New York Times*. They thought that freedom meant absolutely no restrictions at all: rumour, innuendo, and gossip were all dished up as fact, and reporters editorialized according to their leanings. There was no looking over one's shoulder anymore, no fear of persecution.

I tried to explain about the watchdog press councils and libel laws we had in the West, but my explanation didn't tally with their idea of freedom as in democracy and was misinterpreted as unjust criticism of their latest scoop. I am sure the controls on the media by leaders in Russia and places like Kazakhstan are a result of their experience with the free press of those early years: there's a mistrust that refuses to go away.

A question of ethics arose when it transpired that one of our contributors, a Russian who reviewed CDs, was taking money from the company supplying the music as well as accepting his regular per-word pay from us. Our writer thought it was great that two businesses were paying him for the same duties and hadn't particularly made an effort to hide the fact. An American reporter suggested the man should be banned from the newspaper. But ethics was something that had to be taught in the former Soviet Union, and two years of freedom and democracy was not enough time to wipe out old habits. There was even a Russian saying that included something like "people who don't cheat are cheating themselves," and so I decided to give the reviewer a second chance. He provided us with a weekly column and was knowledgeable about the oddest music. It was only when he changed to writing misogynous nightclub reviews that I eventually fired him.

When we were short of editors, Anthony's English mother, Jennifer, would come in to help. She was a matronly woman with grey hair pulled back into a severe bun, no make-up, and glasses perched on a thin, prominent nose. She wore blouses, cardigans, and no-nonsense straight skirts with sensible shoes. She had lived in Russia for about forty years, but remained the quintessential English lady—hiding the grief over the loss of her famous husband, Victor, with a stiff upper lip—and spoke in well-bred Surrey tones. Nothing about the intelligent, straightlaced mother and grandmother in her mid-sixties suggested any connection with a clandestine lifestyle.

Jennifer was a precise editor and demanded that others be similarly skilled and accurate. When I last spoke to her in 2002, she was still churning out *Information Moscow*, a directory that she and her husband Victor first published in 1965. It listed businesses, embassies, government ministries, foreign trade associations, media, international associations, and just about everything else in the city. There was nothing else like it in Moscow then. It was meticulously updated every year with the names of all the new arrivals in embassies and companies. Given the times, only tough, conscientious, dedicated people with good connections could have produced such an accurate book. For years it was the only source for foreigners of telephone numbers and addresses for everything from airlines to art galleries, ministries to hospitals, restaurants to hotels. Almost every foreigner bought a copy, and this enterprise was what generated the Louis family's first money.

Victor and Jennifer also published *Russia—Description and Travel* in 1970, *A Motorist's Guide to the Soviet Union* in 1976, and *The Complete Guide to the Soviet Union* in 1980, which should have been included in every attaché's backpack. These guides were followed by the *Country Road Book,* the *Moscow Street Atlas,* and *150 Town Maps.* To do a travel book prior to 1991 meant very good connections or, as Russians say, a large "umbrella" or "roof." And of course Victor had that.

They were all extremely useful tools for foreign travellers who had been combining their own maps with unreliable local ones for years. Were we issued with these guides before we were sent off on our trips? No we were not, although every embassy stocked the books. Perhaps the West didn't want its spies wandering about carrying maps and information published by Victor Louis. He would have got a good laugh out of it, I'm sure. Then again he didn't have "military barracks," "KGB headquarters," "army base," and "SAM site" marked on his maps as we did on our rice paper substitutes.

Jennifer was an unlikely wife of a suspected KGB agent. She had come to Moscow as a nanny in the fifties for the British naval attaché and his wife and lived with them in a house just off Arbat Street. One day, with a free evening off from work, Jennifer went alone to see a ballet performance at the Bolshoi Theatre. It was pouring rain when she emerged from the theatre, but luckily she had her umbrella. She was standing wondering whether to walk home or take a taxi when a charming man ducked under her umbrella and asked if he could share it. It was Victor, not long out of the gulag. That was their first meeting, and they were married shortly thereafter. Although the Soviet authorities made it difficult for westerners to marry Russians, there was no objection to Victor's wedding.

Had Victor deliberately chosen Jennifer because she could provide a perfect cover for his activities? Judging by her children's looks (not Anthony's, who resembled his father in a photo I was shown), she'd been attractive as a young woman with fine features, fair skin, and wavy light brown hair.

Drinking blueberry tea with her at the Peredilkino dacha, it was hard to imagine the Jennifer of forty years earlier who had decided to leave her prim and proper job, marry a Russian of unknown persuasion, and live in Russia. Was it pluck, foolishness, or just a sense of adventure? It must have created quite a stir in Moscow's small diplomatic world.

She learned to speak Russian well, remained a Protestant, christened the three boys, and threw herself into her family, travelling with her husband to research their guidebooks, entertaining, editing, and supporting the International Women's Club. Her biggest triumph was her work towards the re-establishment of St. Andrew's Anglican Church in Moscow. The church had long been used as a recording studio when the first service in seventy-one years was held there, following the fall of Communism.

Seemingly undaunted by the breakup of the Soviet Union and the death of her husband in 1992, Jennifer continued to put out *Information Moscow* and then *Information CIS and Baltics*. Gradually in the growing free market economy, other directories sprang up in Moscow and vied with her guides for advertising, but none had the history and accuracy of *Information Moscow*.

Information Moscow was printed in England. In the midst of my time in Moscow, Jennifer asked me if I would carry some of the proofs back with me while I was on a visit to the UK and hand them to her oldest son who lived in London. We agreed on a meeting place in Guildford, halfway between London and where I would be staying. I hung around in a W.H. Smith bookstore on Guildford High Street whiling away time, looking at books until our meeting. I was wearing a raincoat with large pockets, big enough to hold books—or so someone must have thought. I felt myself surrounded by store detectives. They were in front of me, behind me, and on either side. Or was it my imagination after spending so much time in Moscow stores followed by suspicious clerks? Maybe I had caressed the merchandise too much and looked at it too long? I may have been acting a bit strangely after months on the Eastern front.

I fled the store and walked towards our designated meeting place. I held the brown paper package in my hand and suddenly realized I was meeting the oldest son of a world-famous spy on a corner in England to hand over a package. I imagined the headline: "Canadian diplomat's wife caught in espionage ring." Suppose all those people I had seen in W.H. Smith's were British Secret Service? On the cobblestones outside Marks and Spencer, I handed over a package to a handsome young man, and in due course the fall edition of *Information Moscow* arrived in our office.

Blueberry tea always reminds me of Jennifer. When I visited her, she still had a decidedly English garden with lawns, flowers, shrubs, and trees that would have been equally at home in the grounds of her other home in Surrey, albeit patrolled by Siberian guard dogs. The indoor swimming pool was drained, and Victor's huge collection of books had spilled out from the library even into this space. One could sense how vital the house had been years earlier when the children were young, Victor's work had been in full swing, and the cream of Moscow's foreign residents had been entertained.

During her marriage I can only guess that Jennifer ignored Victor's well-known title of "famous spy." Perhaps, like me, she enjoyed the role of spy's wife (although in a more premier league).

Being a spy did interfere a little with my being a journalist. Or was it the other way around? One night I had to cover a ceremony at the British embassy. We needed the photo and story for the next day's paper. I took a shot of the occasion, but then had to stay on for a while to have dinner with the ambassador. Between courses I stole out of the embassy with my film and down to the perimeter of the grounds where I knew my driver was parked. By then it was dark. "Take this to the paper and then come back for me," I said, handing him the film through the railings. At that moment a man sitting in a car parked across the road took a photo. It looked as though I had been caught in some clandestine act by the secret police. I was paranoid about the incident for a while. I didn't know whether it would affect my diplomatic status or just my journalistic one. In the end, I never heard any more about it. It must have been relegated to the "future suspects" file.

19

October Uprising

In September 1993 President Boris Yeltsin decreed that parliament was dissolved and new parliamentary elections would be held in December, as well as a referendum on a new constitution. This move was the culmination of a power struggle between Yeltsin and parliament that began the year before when the president introduced his "shock therapy" free market reforms, which had become widely unpopular. Besides being in violation of the existing constitution, dissolving parliament was the last straw for hard-line Communist and nationalistic parliamentarians; it set Yeltsin on a collision course with MPs, Vice-President Alexander Rutskoi, and the speaker of parliament, Ruslan Khasbulatov. When the president refused to reverse his decision, the anti-Yeltsin faction seized the White House, the prominent building beside the Moscow River where parliament was held, and barricaded itself inside.

Living conditions for a large part of the Russian population had deteriorated alarmingly since 1991 when all the monetary safety nets of the Soviet Union had been rudely removed. Over half the population had become impoverished as savings were liquidated by hyperinflation, and jobs disappeared. Life expectancy dropped as the health service collapsed, and people drank themselves to death. It became the survival of the fittest (and the not-so-fit). Artists, writers, road sweepers, office workers, shop assistants, teachers, pensioners, the educated, the uneducated, and families in general were desperately trying to make ends meet. Only insiders, mobsters, black marketers, con artists, prostitutes, illegal moneychangers, corrupt officials, clever schemers, and dubious risk takers were thriving in the new Russia. They became the new elite. Some time later they were the oligarchs, the millionaires, the billionaires, the new upper class, the new middle class. Generally they were referred to as New Russians. Poor Russians called them "mafia." Hard currency began leaving Russia in bagfuls. In 1993 the majority of these movers and shakers were in their twenties and early thirties.

When Yeltsin declared his coup against parliament in the name of democracy, it was the little guys, the moms and pops, the ordinary Russians, supported by Vice-President Rutskoi and parliamentary deputies, who cried foul. They were broke and sick of democracy. Very quickly they were joined by Communists, nationalists, Stalinists, and neo-Nazis. Everyone was broiling for a fight. From Tuesday, September 28 to Saturday, October 2 they battled with the tough military riot troops on Moscow's busy main inner road, the Garden Ring, trying to reach the sealed-off White House inside of which remained the vice-president, the speaker, and MPs along with the cooks, cleaners, secretaries, ordinary folk, and odds and sods who were against Yeltsin. For days they stayed there. First the electricity was cut off, then the water. They had little food, and no clean clothes. Every day the police used more and more force on the street demonstrators as they tried to close off the main circular road with barricades.

During the first days of the crisis we were receiving regular telephone tips at the newspaper from our reporters on the scene. Ministry of the Interior riot police, we heard, were on the move against demonstrators near a metro station just behind the White House. These riot troops, known as OMON, were a frightening bunch. Kalashnikovs in hand, they wore dark-blue-and-black camouflage uniforms and black ski masks. Unidentifiable, they could do what they wanted, and did. They meant business and in chasing protesters, they often beat innocent bystanders. These were Yeltsin's men.

I always passed on the latest information to Sam. One night he was at a reception at the residence of the American Ambassador with the rest of Moscow's foreign and military attachés and Russian guests when OMON used particular force against anti-Yeltsin protesters. Our reporters felt things had deteriorated to a point of finality. Something bad was going to happen. I searched for the telephone number of the ambassador's residence. I phoned the embassy, but couldn't get the number from the staff. Then I found it in *Information Moscow*. It turned out to be for the kitchen of the residence, but it was good enough. In my best Russian I told the cook, or whoever had answered the phone, that I had to speak to the Canadian military attaché immediately. It was an emergency. After a long wait, my husband came to the phone. Called to a phone in the kitchen of the American Ambassador's residence, he was wondering what on earth was going on.

Returning to the reception, he quickly spread the word among all the NATO attachés that it looked like the balloon was about to go up. Because of the Russian presence, they slipped away surreptitiously a few at a time. They did not want to miss the latest in the country's battle for democracy. I worked late editing our stories, combining them with wire stories, and carefully avoided the Garden Ring as I drove home. I should have liked to be there myself, but it was just the beginning of the battle. There was time yet for me to get involved. My spy training would help me handle myself and survive the ensuing events.

On October 2, Sam and I walked along the ring road among the demonstrators, and that's when the age and circumstances of the majority of the crowd struck me. It was a Saturday afternoon, and hundreds of ordinary Russians in their forties, fifties, sixties, and up—the men in inexpensive fall jackets and some with flat caps and the women in well-worn coats and sensible shoes—were in the middle of the road busily gathering piles of rocks, pressing a powdery substance into small pieces of metal pipe, and preparing Molotov cocktails: glass bottles filled with gasoline with a piece of cloth stuffed in the neck. The idea was to light the rag with matches and throw it. In fact all the weapons were the throwing kind. The demonstrators knew the OMON troops were lining up in riot gear about 200 yards down the road, and they would soon be meeting them.

I had never seen a Molotov cocktail up close before, but had heard about the Russians using them effectively against German tanks during the Second World War. It was a very primitive weapon (named after Stalin's deputy, Molotov), and people busied themselves making them on that fall day in Moscow as though they had done it all their lives. I realized as I took photographs that some of them were old enough to have been in the war. Most were too busy to look up at the camera.

As the protesters worked and nonchalantly smoked cigarettes among the primitive weaponry, life was going on as normal on the city sidewalks around them. Muscovites were out browsing the stores, as they did most Saturdays, though in more of a hurry than usual. They did not want to be caught between the troops and the demonstrators. The ragtag army looked as if it had already done its weekend purchasing, judging by the plastic bags at their feet. In Russia, important events had always been secondary to shopping. Once it had been because there was nothing in the stores. In 1993 there was plenty, but many ordinary people couldn't afford the high prices of the new super stores and instead spent time searching in small shops and kiosks for low-cost food and clothing. Even in the markets prices had spiralled.

The protesters were so strongly against Yeltsin's reforms—his dissolving of parliament and his rule by decree—that they were prepared to do battle. They were husbands and wives, mothers and fathers. All of them might have looked very much at home picking potatoes in a field, stacking wheat, or just cleaning house. There were few young people, and those we saw seemed to be relatives.

We walked a few more yards down the ring road towards the Ministry of Foreign Affairs. The view was ominous. Lined up behind barricades were rows of armed OMON forces, some three or four deep. They eyed us suspiciously. A photograph of them was out of the question. I felt they would have ripped the film from my camera. They'd probably heard talk of the Molotov cocktails awaiting them and were more fired up than usual.

We'd seen enough and walked the few blocks home where we put on CNN for the finale. Unlike the coup d'état in 1991 that saw the end of Communism, this October crisis was being covered by the media. The West saw the encounter as a further struggle for democratic reform in Russia and wholeheartedly supported Yeltsin. The clash came later in the afternoon, and OMON easily dispersed the protesters. It seemed like only a matter of time before civil war broke out in Russia.

The anti-Yeltsin parliamentarians, still shut in the White House, had already appointed Vice-President Rutskoi as acting president. Rutskoi had been a military hero in the Soviet Union's Afghanistan conflict in the eighties, and Yeltsin's vice-president since 1991. It was estimated that there were about 500 people inside the building with him. However, the Russian capital is known to be riddled with underground tunnels, some secret, some not so secret, and the local media were reporting that people were escaping from the White House to safety via this means. Other reports said tunnels from the White House led to Kievskaya Metro Station and a dock on the Moscow River, among other places, and had Yeltsin's forces fighting their way up them.

Whatever the facts really were, the next day, Sunday, October 3 saw thousands of anti-Yeltsin demonstrators on the Garden Ring, and the mood was ugly. This time we walked down small side streets to watch the protesters overrun Yeltsin's OMON forces in one direction, then return and break through riot police cordons at the White House. The crowd was armed with more than homemade weapons. Pistols, rifles, and machine guns were fired, and bullets hit buildings in the American Embassy compound, including the homes of American military attachés. The forces opposing Yeltsin commandeered trucks and rammed through the front of Moscow's thirty-storey modern-skyscraper City Hall. Again there was gunfire, and the first victims of many over the next two days were claimed.

There was a strange and dangerous atmosphere. Eerily, security forces seemed to fade away. It was a phony calm before the storm. We returned to our apartment a few blocks from the White House, and I phoned the newspaper. Anthony had a skeleton staff putting out a special Sunday edition because Yeltsin had now declared a state of emergency. I explained that I was a little tied up, and he understood. He knew what the job of a Canadian attaché and spouse was. We picked up Sam's white Zhiguli and parked it closer to the action, but in a safe spot in a neighbouring apartment complex with easy access. We mingled with the demonstrators now around the White House, trying to look as inconspicuous as possible. Yeltsin's opponents thought westerners were as responsible as the president for their miserable existence after the fall of Communism. We didn't speak in English, but only uttered Russian words. I'm sure we didn't fool anyone. We didn't dare take photos or videotape the scene.

Although the crowd had marched on police and caused damage at city hall, at times they didn't feel as frightening as, say, the average out-of-control British football hooligans. They weren't there just for the sake of causing a riot; they were angry because they genuinely thought they had been mistreated and neglected.

We made our way to the rear of the White House not far from

the compound of the American Embassy, where residents and embassy staff had been gathered together in the gym, and even the military attachés were not allowed outside. Later, an American said it was more frightening being in there and not knowing what was going on outside—especially when the group heard the gunfire.

The crowd was beginning to agitate and wonder what to do next. They all knew that Yeltsin would not give up so easily and was planning something. Then from a balcony at the back of the White House, Vice-President Rutskoi appeared. He gave a fiery speech, urging the crowd to take over the television centre about six kilometres away and broadcast to the nation.

There were half a dozen trucks and buses parked around the White House that had been abandoned by police and government guards. It seemed too easy. Stirred by the speech, Yeltsin's opponents—dozens of men, many carrying Kalashnikovs—poured into the vehicles and began heading for the Ostankino TV buildings. We ran to get our car and joined the parade. It was at that moment that pro-Yeltsin forces, OMON, and the Kremlin guards realized what would happen if the protesters took over the air. They leapt into their armoured personnel carriers (APCs) and trucks and joined the chase. The race was on.

Along the Garden Ring we all drove in a sort of formation. The anti-Yeltsin rebels and pro-Yeltsin forces were sometimes neck and neck, sometimes waving at each other. We were behind them. I think oncoming cars just drove on to the sidewalk. That's normal in Moscow when motorists are faced with a crisis on the roads.

A few of the pro-Yeltsin forces arrived just seconds before the rebels, and less than 100 of them managed to race inside and take up positions. We parked and cautiously approached one of the buildings of the television complex. It was dark by then.

People were milling about. It was hard to see if they were spectators, journalists, or demonstrators. We were only about fifty feet away when we heard the blast of a grenade hitting the building, followed by shooting. We dropped to the ground and realized that Yeltsin's opponents had decided to rush the building. Heavy and small arms fire continued. People had been hit. Bleeding, they came staggering across the street. Others, not so lucky, just lay on the sidewalk. Ambulances arrived on the scene, and doctors and medics raced out during lulls in the firing and loaded both the dead and wounded. There was shouting from around the ambulances and screaming from the wounded. Friends were helping injured friends towards the waiting vehicles. Medics couldn't go into the middle of the battle, but they drove as close as they dared. Bullets were flying everywhere. The road and sidewalk were splattered with blood. We watched from behind a small cluster of bushes, which was ridiculous because they wouldn't have protected us from anything. We were just lucky nothing came in our direction. Among the killed and wounded were journalists (six killed, nine wounded) who had gone into the building with the first wave of protesters. Of course Yeltsin's forces had opened fire on everyone. The protesters apparently had a rocket-propelled grenade and a mortar as well as their Kalashnikovs.

Then we heard a familiar sound: APCs belonging to Yeltsin's security forces were coming up the road. Behind us was the park in which stood the huge Ostankino television tower, one of the largest communications towers in the world. The APCs approached, firing. The tracer bullets were going over our heads. Powerful lights on top of the APCs swept back and forth through the park. The big guns had been called in because by this time the anti-Yeltsin group had managed to capture the first floor of the building.

We crept back and found a wide ditch. There were other people already in there. They too had anticipated what the APCs would do, and sure enough we watched the first one crash through the bushes where we had been minutes earlier. It came towards us, but swerved at the last minute as the soldiers on board spotted some people running across the park. It fired bullets in their direction. The light on the APC was searching the area where we were crouched. At that moment we weren't "foreign diplomats"; we would be seen as fleeing rebels. It was war, and we were caught right in the middle. Even if the APC trundled over the wide ditch without firing on us, it would have crushed us.

Then lucky for us, someone fired on the APC from the TV centre, and it turned towards the building and poured bullets into it. The other APCs stopped and did the same.

We stayed in the ditch for a couple of hours, watching the spectacle unfold. The road was strewn with shattered buses and trucks that had carried the demonstrators from the White House. Ambulances continued to arrive, and drivers, doctors, and medics worked together picking up the victims, bundling them inside, and pulling quickly away. It was dangerous work and probably unpaid: health care services, including the wages of doctors and other workers, had been hard hit by Yeltsin's reforms.

We had to report back to the embassy, and it was already after midnight so during a lull in the fighting we climbed out of the ditch and, crouching, slowly backed farther and farther into the park until we reached the road on the other side. Our eyes never left the direction of the patrolling APCs. We then made our way back to our car.

Ambassador Kinsman was waiting for news, and we told him our impressions of what we had seen to add to his account of events for Ottawa's consumption. We had received only a broad outline from Laurie Dean our basement sleuth, as to the needs of military intelligence. As usual, he let the attachés on the ground make their own decisions. That night we were the eyes and ears of not only the Canadian military but, because they were shut in their embassy and not allowed on the streets, the US military as well. Our reports would have been received by Ottawa and then fed directly into the intelligence pipeline to Washington. western foreign policy-makers were eager to learn whether Yeltsin was going to emerge the winner or loser in the crisis.

We knew there would be a high toll of deaths and injury from the events at Ostankino, but worse was yet to come; Russia's armed forces decided to enter the fracas. Diplomats and journalists had been speculating about the military's delay in coming to Yeltsin's aide, and had concluded the reluctance was due to painful memories of the army's participation in the aborted coup of 1991. But as dawn broke on October 4, an elite army tank division rolled down Moscow's main Kutusovsky Prospekt (the road that ran parallel to where we lived) towards the White House. The assault on the Russian parliament to remove the entrenched rebels from the building had begun.

By the time I went in to work in the morning, the white parliament building was under bombardment from tanks stationed outside the Ukraine Hotel across the Moscow River. Although there were tanks and APCs on the Garden Ring and surrounding the White House, crowds of people were allowed to watch. They stood on Kalininsky Bridge at the end of Kutusovsky, with heads following the fire back and forth.

I learned at the paper that more than sixty people had been killed at Ostankino the night before, and hundreds had been wounded. One of our reporters had been arrested by government forces, and we were still looking for his whereabouts.

I left work for a while to drive home, park my car, and walk to watch the action at the White House. The tank assault was accompanied by almost constant sniper fire from the upper stories of several downtown Moscow buildings. By now several spectators, including teenagers, watching the exciting firefight from the bridge had been killed, and many had been injured. But the rest remained undeterred and in the open. Two people watching the fighting from windows in the Ukraine Hotel had also been killed. Red-tracer machine gun fire poured into the White House and was immediately returned by the defenders, who had managed to acquire anti-tank guns. There were loud booms as the military's elite *tankists* zeroed in on the latter. Bullets and other weaponry flew over the spectators' heads. There is a frightening streak of fatalism in Russians that I didn't care to share at that moment, and I found myself a tree from which to survey the scene.

Russians were watching because there was so much at stake between winners and losers: those whose lives had been shattered by the shock of the past two years and wanted the pain to stop and those who had experienced a bit of extra freedom and, for better or worse, wanted reforms to continue. They were also watching because of the spectacle of a crack Russian tank regiment firing into the parliament building containing hundreds of fellow Russians in the middle of Moscow. They were sombre and a bit ashamed about Yeltsin's style of democracy: a western journalist I'd seen making notes on the bridge was chased away from a public phone booth near where I was standing after spectators rudely wrenched the phone out of his hands and shouted at him. He looked scared, and I suddenly felt vulnerable.

The White House was burning. It was a sad sight. Tank rounds were hitting it continually now and several floors and the far end of the building were in flames. Gunfire from the building was becoming intermittent.

I went back to the newspaper office. We were trying to get the paper to the presses earlier than usual as an 11 P.M. curfew had been imposed. According to the wire services and our reporters, people in the White House were surrendering and leaving the building. Rutskoi and Khasbulatov were on their way to Lefortovo prison, one of the worst prisons in Moscow. Still, a few people didn't give up, and snipers continued firing on troops from various buildings near the parliament.

Sam, who was unaware that I was at the scene too, watched the fighting closer to the White House. A few tanks passed him near the end of Novy Arbat Street as if leaving the scene. Suddenly a sniper opened fire from a floor high on an apartment block. The tanks halted. Then their turrets swung quickly towards the offending fire. They blasted the side of the building away, and the sniper was no more. Then they continued on their way past an armoured car on its side, a smashed bus, and thousands of spectators.

Some of the talk at the paper was that the whole incident might have been an ingenious sting by Yeltsin to end the siege at the White House and, in doing so, round up and dispose of as many members of the opposition as possible. Perhaps that's why on Sunday night, before the events at Ostankino, riot troops hadn't used tear gas, water cannons, or extra force to try to block the crowd from reaching the White House. Had the security forces abandoned trucks in front of the White House complete with keys for the rebels to use? And why were there no roadblocks on the way to Ostankino?

Russian reporters talked excitedly of hundreds being killed in the White House, and of the secret removal of bodies from the charred building under the cover of darkness. Others had them being taken down the tunnels and away by boat. Sam saw the bodies of at least 20 unfortunate spectators laid out near the bridge and dozens beside the White House. In the end the official death toll was about 150, including those at Ostankino, with almost 1,000 wounded.

As the reports came in, and the editors sorted out fact from fiction, it turned out all our young Russian journalists were pro-Yeltsin. They made it clear in their stories they had little sympathy for Rutskoi, that as far as they were concerned his "Communist" followers had got what they deserved, and it was no use crying over a pounded parliament when democracy was at stake. Market reformers, Russian liberals, and the president would have been proud of them. And we had a deadline.

Yeltsin's 11 P.M. curfew on everyone except troops, police, and emergency services meant that we had to finish the paper by 10 P.M. and drive it to the press before the appointed deadline. It was an impossible feat. Every night we scrambled just to meet a 1 A.M. deadline. And now we had enough stories to fill two newspapers.

We had found our English reporter. He had been arrested and thrown in jail with a whole host of other people. The cells were crowded. We sent someone over to the police station to get him released. He told us that the most frightening thing that had happened to him was being forced to give the police a blood sample. Someone came around with one needle attached to a long rubber tube. They went from person to person filling little vials, using the same needle all the time. He was worried about infection for a long time after that.

I managed to leave the office at 10:45. There was only 15 minutes to curfew, and a half-hour drive home. The paper was finished, and the driver ran out of the building with it at the same time that I left. Some staff had decided that they would stay at the office overnight rather than risk running into the police cordons thrown up in the city.

I got into my red two-door Lada and started off. It was quite a long drive to the other side of the city, past Moscow State University on Sparrow Hill, overlooking the Moscow River and Olympic Park.

Suddenly I saw people moving about on the road ahead. Being so close to curfew, I was the only vehicle on the road. I was waved down by a whole bevy of OMON troops.

I stopped, and a hooded soldier approached the car. I could only see his eyes glinting behind the balaclava by the light of my own car headlights. The scenario was reminiscent of our training in Canada, but with two important differences: I was on my own, and the man walking towards me was deadly serious, part of a force I had seen in lethal action.

I rolled down my window all the way, not just a tiny notch as we had been taught. This was no time to say, "I am a diplomat," and expect to be waved through. He had already seen the red diplomatic plates on my car and still thrust his Kalashnikov at me demanding, "Show me your ID."

I should have been prepared for this moment with my ID at the ready, but instead I had to search around in my deep handbag for my special diplomatic card. It seemed to take forever, but the training I had received in Ottawa really kicked in because I wasn't feeling unduly nervous about the encounter. I had already faced Kalashnikovs in Chechnya and knew that calmness was the best solution. Perhaps I was over-trained.

When he saw my special ID, I think he had to ponder what the wife of a diplomat and a military attaché was doing driving home alone at ten minutes to curfew. Was the situation worse for me if he suspected I might be spying? I had a fleeting thought about our English reporter's experience in a Russian prison cell. I was beginning to feel feisty. It would not have been an easy arrest.

But he looked at my ID only for a moment and then let me go. I continued on my way, passed some huge official residences beside the Moscow River where dignitaries like Richard Nixon and Yasser Arafat stayed when they were visiting Yeltsin, and then followed the river for about four or five kilometres. On a dark stretch of the road I was stopped again. This time it was closer to 11 P.M., and I could see the OMON soldier was debating whether to haul me in. But I was lucky, and he let me go with just a warning. "Go home *now*."

When I pulled into the parking lot of our apartment building, I was met by the group of men who guarded it. They were not only amazed to see me, but angry too. Probably they had reasoned that everyone in their building was accounted for and didn't take kindly to losing control, especially during a government curfew. I had told them several times that I worked for a newspaper, but they never really got the message. Meanwhile Sam was not amused by my appearance after the curfew either. I knew he wouldn't have been happy if I had called from the local jail—even if I could.

As it was, all our efforts to get good stories were in vain. The next day we found the paper had been censored. There were white spaces where stories had been cut out.

But it had been done in a haphazard fashion because mysteriously some of the stories about the uprising remained. The driver told us that when he arrived at the press, it was already after curfew. The censor was waiting, but the Russian papers were his first priority. Because he didn't speak a word of English, he had to guess what was offensive in the *Tribune* and what wasn't. The driver had slept at the press because of the danger of being rounded up by OMON.

The same routine occurred for the next few nights, but we managed to get out earlier, and I didn't encounter any more roadblocks on the way home. The driver was also getting better at avoiding the censor. A couple of times he managed to slip by the man's office door as he lay slumped asleep in his chair.

It had taken eight hours from the start of the tanks bombarding the White House to the surrender of the leaders of the rebels inside. The general in charge of the tank regiment that fired into the White House came to our house for dinner the day after the attack. It was an invitation that had been extended some time before, and we wondered if he would cancel.

There was so much interest in meeting him from foreign military attachés and diplomats—most wanted to know why there had been some reluctance at first on the part of the Russian Army to support Yeltsin—that we'd had to change the evening from a dinner party to a buffet. The feeling among the guests was that the army's top generals had resisted either out of sympathy for fellow Afghan veteran Rutskoi, or they were not sure if Yeltsin had popular support.

But our Russian guest was a pragmatic man. As far as he was concerned, he had done what he had to do and had won the day. He couldn't be lured into talking politics. We drank toasts, and the general proposed one to his *tankists* whose rounds had hardly caused any structural damage to the outside of the building because "we aimed for the windows." As a soldier who had been ordered to do battle by his president, he couldn't be faulted for the deaths that had occurred as a result. All the military attachés present agreed on that.

Although the general seemed in good humour and unfazed by the previous day's bombardment, inside he might have been feeling a little differently: a few months later the chief of the armed forces said that his generals still felt bitter because they had been forced to help solve the problems created by political confrontation. Some soldiers who took part in the attack on the White House attempted to conceal their role in the assault out of fear of retaliation.

As Yeltsin had decreed, new parliamentary elections were held on December 12, and Russians voted on a new constitution. It passed, and presidential powers significantly increased. One of the first acts of the new parliament was to grant amnesty to the leaders of the anti-Yeltsin campaign, and in February they were released from jail. The same year the White House was restored by a Turkish company at a cost of $300 million US.

Imprisonment didn't end Rutskoi's political ambitions. He founded a one-man political party and unsuccessfully contested for a seat in parliament in 1995 and for the presidency in 1996. The same year he was elected governor of Kursk Region. He held this position until 2000, when he was banned from running in re-elections on a technicality. Khasbalatov, a Chechen, quit politics, returned to his earlier profession as an economics teacher, and became a leading critic of Russia's role in Chechnya.

20

Art of Diplomacy

After the fall of the Soviet Union, the Baltic countries were quick to reject Russia, the hated occupier, and everything Russian. Latvians, Lithuanians, and even Estonians made life uncomfortable for the large ethnic Russian population left behind. Many of these Russians had never known another homeland. Language, immigration, and work laws added to their misery, as did another result of independence—the returnees.

Returnees were mainly the grown-up children of the thousands of people who fled to America from the Baltics in the early forties when the Soviets kicked out the German occupiers and made the countries part of the Soviet Union. So, for example, a town planner from Seattle could easily become the Latvian foreign minister or even prime minister, and a policeman from Chicago the chief of the defence staff. And they returned with great chips on their shoulders—all disliking Russians.

I had lived in Russia long enough and had had enough contact with Russian people through my work and travel to have become pretty defensive when I saw this type of behaviour. And I saw it in spades when we returned to Riga in 1993 for a conference on defence issues and visits to a former Soviet base which had now become a Latvian military base. The tone was set at the conference. Every new ambassador to the Baltics was present as were all their military attachés. Canada was still represented from Moscow, and it soon became obvious why this couldn't continue—the new Latvian ministers were American accented and anti-Russian. Canada needed to come to the new Baltic countries with fresh eyes.

During the briefings about the Russian troops still stationed at their old bases in the Baltics, several questions were asked of the new prime minister and the new foreign minister by foreign ambassadors. The replies were civil except when it came to a question from the Russian Ambassador, a large man with glasses and an intellectual air. The question, which was innocuous enough, and asked in English, was answered in a terse, dismissive tone.

He ignored the put-down and asked a second question later on. He seemed to expect no less from the Latvian officials. The Russian did have sympathizers among some of the more experienced diplomats present, and I remember the Swiss Ambassador remarking on the rudeness of the reply.

During lunch we were seated in the large dining hall of a restaurant. While there were four or five tables of ten or twelve conference attendees, the Russian Ambassador and his military attaché found themselves seated at a table for two in a corner, like naughty schoolchildren.

It was hard to comment or say much about the American returnees as there were always two or three American military attachés within hearing distance. On more than one occasion Sam threw me a warning look. "Just don't mention it!"

The Chicago police officer who was now in charge of the military was exactly like the caricatured American soldier who carried a knife in his belt that he called "Mikey" in the Tom Hanks and John Candy comedy, *Volunteers*. The policeman was about six feet two and dressed from head to toe in American fatigues with a cap pulled low over his eyebrows. He walked with his hand on his belt and was extremely serious. He didn't talk. He barked.

And what he was barking at were forty young Latvians, also dressed in American fatigues, marching towards us to the sound of their own swinging voices, American style. "We are soldiers da da da / We defend Latvia."

I don't know what the Russian Ambassador and his military attaché thought, but I could guess. Here they were on a former Soviet base, watching an American-style army marching across their former territory, complete with US Army uniforms. I suppose the Latvians had to start somewhere and now along with the other Baltic States, they had marched right into NATO and the European Union. We found out in Riga that Canada had also supplied uniforms to the new army, but there had been a mix-up—the sizes that had been supplied were children's sizes and useless. What had Ottawa been thinking?

Michael Bell was the Canadian Ambassador to Moscow from 1990 to 1993. He lived with his wife, Christine, in residence at the embassy on Starokonyushenny Pereulok (Old Stable Lane) just off Arbat Street. They decided they wanted some privacy from the Moscow expats who spilled out of the basement social club into the back of the embassy on warm Friday nights and drank Canadian beer, so they built a high brick wall with a substantial gate around their garden. The garden contained the only grass in the compound, so the expats were left sitting on lawn chairs in the driveway.

Bell was replaced in January 1993 by Jeremy Kinsman, a more laid-back individual. He arrived in Moscow with his second wife, Hana, a tall, vivacious, sports-loving Czech. Hana had escaped with her daughter from Czechoslovakia during the Cold War. As Kinsman had served as deputy minister for political and international security with the Department of Foreign Affairs, this liaison with a refuge from a Warsaw Pact country might have blotted his record. It didn't. Some people with a certain unapproachable poise and stature are beyond doubtful questions. Besides, he was too bright to be overlooked, and he subsequently became ambassador in

Italy, in the UK, and then to the EU. His wife spoke Russian, and together they were perfect for the Moscow of the early to mid-nineties. They opened up the garden gate in the summer and shared the lawn of their residence on Friday nights.

The Canadian embassy employed the student sons and daughters of Canadian staff during the long summer holidays. The first summer James worked at odd jobs like weeding the ambassador's garden, cutting the grass, and attending to shrubs on the embassy grounds. The second and third summers he was employed in the visa section of the embassy and did some computer programming.

Working at the embassy as a locally engaged employee was Heidi Hollinger, in her early twenties, from Montreal. Attractive and outgoing, Hollinger was popular with all of the young embassy staff, both Russian and English speaking. But she caused a stir among the diplomatic hierarchy when she became involved with extreme nationalist politician Vladimir Zhirinovsky.

In 1993 Heidi was probably Moscow's only female inline skater: I saw her roller-blade down the busy eight-lane Novy Arbat Street in the city's centre, her head deep into a magazine. This was not only daring, it was dangerous: the road had several uncovered manholes. For this exercise she wore very short, black shorts and a black halter. Muscovites were agog.

It was this kind of free-spirited behaviour that probably attracted Zhirinovsky, the well-known loudmouth of Russian right-wing politics. Hollinger became his official photographer and also the photographer for his ultra-nationalist friends.

The first I knew of her liaison with Zhirinovsky was when Heidi came to the *Moscow Tribune* office clutching a pile of photographs she had taken. The quality of most of the photos was not good, but the subject matter was startling. The photographs were of the politician fooling around in his underwear in a bathroom.

She said that *Time* magazine was interested in the shots, and I could see why: the photographs certainly highlighted the political party leader's boorish character.

I had to decide whether our paper wanted to buy them. I was cautious. We were published at the Russian state press in Moscow and had to be careful about Mr. Zhirinovsky and his accomplices. That was my thought as an editor. As a diplomat I was wondering how the embassy would view the explicit photos and the story from Hollinger about how she had obtained them. (She was very open about how the politician had been grabbing her as she pressed the shutter.)

If it had been Yeltsin in his underwear, I could not have resisted, but in the end I chose tamer shots from her selection. *Time* published the controversial ones.

The photographs of Zhirinovsky garnered a lot of publicity for the young Canadian. Armed with charm and *chutzpah,* she became a well-known and accomplished photographer in Moscow. When Alexandre Trudeau, son of Pierre Trudeau, went to Moscow to write a series of articles on Russia for *Maclean's* in 2004, it was Hollinger who introduced him to the local scene. And it was she who was invited to take photographs of his brother Justin's wedding in Montreal in 2005.

High-level visits by government ministers from Ottawa always caused excitement at the embassy. It was 1992, a window of opportunity for both Canada and Russia, and everyone was trying to make a good impression—the Russians on us, and we on the Russians. People on both sides dressed up for events, smiled at receptions, and behaved carefully and courteously. Russian officials were learning not to necessarily kiss other men, as was their custom, but to take the opportunity to buss their western counterparts' wives instead. They were even producing their own wives at parties to receive the foreign diplomats' irritating peck-peck and sometimes peck-peck-peck to the cheeks.

For a foreign official to arrive in Moscow looking too informal, too under-dressed, while the hosts were trying so hard was an insult. So when the minister of foreign affairs, Barbara McDougall, walked off the plane at Sheremetyevo-2 Airport wearing a tracksuit, both the embassy staff and the Russians were dismayed. She must have thought she was in Saskatchewan. The Russians were turned out in their best suits. It always amazed me that despite money hardships, lack of electricity, and cramped living quarters, most Muscovites emerged onto the streets every morning with neat hair and in pressed, clean clothing.

From Moscow the foreign minister wanted to fly to India, where she was due to host a luncheon, and she wanted to fly the quickest route possible, which was over Iran. The only problem was her aircraft had not received a clearance to fly over that country. That didn't trouble McDougall—after dinner with Ambassador Michael Bell, she went to bed, still determined to fly to India by way of Iran in the early hours of the next morning. The ambassador and the military attachés were left with the problem of getting clearance. Because Iran was sleeping, and no one was answering the phone, calls were placed to Iranian Ambassadors in other parts of the world, including Ottawa.

Shortly after midnight, someone was delegated to wake the minister and tell her that she would probably not make her luncheon in India the next day. McDougall was not pleased and still emphatic that she was going anyway. The aircrew, flying a military aircraft, albeit a small executive jet, said they weren't willing to take the risk. The ambassador, now willing to try anything to get rid of the minister, woke up the Iranian Ambassador in Moscow and accused him of creating an international incident. Stunned and stung, both the Iranian and Canadian Ambassadors called everyone they knew in Iran.

Finally the plane took off, still without clearance, but with everyone who mattered in Iran aware that a Canadian aircraft carrying the minister of foreign affairs was going to fly through their air space within a couple of hours. I would still have felt uneasy if I'd been that crew.

Curiously, during this period, the old Elton John recording of "The Bitch Is Back" had been heard emanating from the embassy's sound system. "Let's hope we don't have to play that song again for long while," said a staffer, the day after the minister's departure.

21

Brief Reunion

Every good spy needs to be debriefed now and again. That's why all the Canadian military attachés from the former Soviet Union countries and Eastern Bloc countries gathered in a small town in Germany once a year.

The first time we met, in 1992, was in the southern town of Lahr that for years had been the location of a Canadian military base. By the time of the second gathering, in 1993, the Canadians had closed both this base and the one near the beautiful spa city of Baden-Baden, and we assembled at a US military base at Ramstein.

The meetings were like reunions as we once again met the attachés and their wives from Czechoslovakia, Italy, Spain, and Turkey with whom we had trained at the language school. In addition, the attachés from Hungary, Poland, and other nearby countries attended. By the time of the second meeting we had all changed a great deal, now so much more knowledgeable, and either liking the country in which we were living very much, or loathing it. Sam and I were in the first category.

Intelligence experts from Ottawa gave briefings from the outside world and then it was the attachés' turn. The senior intelligence fraternity is a strange lot and Canada's is no exception. Realizing that trained attachés immediately begin to know a lot more about the country they are working in and its inhabitants than they do, the senior spooks have to devise ways to keep control. One way is to appear less interested in what you have to say, or less friendly.

The photographs we took were sent back to them and they always removed the ones that they deemed interesting and sent back those they thought might be useful to us as "holiday snapshots." Most of the time we were shooting the same sites that had been photographed many times previously, and Ottawa was looking for any changes. All attachés had been told of other spies who had taken the first-ever photo of this or the first-ever photo of that. It was all mostly luck—being in the right place at the right time. But now, in Russia, "firsts" were becoming a thing of the past: we were beginning to see all their weapons and they were even on sale to us at bargain prices.

Sam was the first Westerner to fly in a MiG-31 and had also flown in a MiG-29 within a year of arriving in Russia. Later, during a tour of a Mikoyan museum in Moscow, we found Sam's name on a new plaque commemorating his MiG-31 flight alongside a Canadian flag.

The flight took place during Russia's first "open" commercial and military air show, which was held at Zhukovsky. As he approached the fighter, Sam put his camera inside his flying suit for the MiG ride. The Russian pilot saw him and warned, "You might get into trouble." Fortunately, Sam had taken James with him to watch the flight and he followed his dad up the cockpit ladder to take photos. No one said anything.

We both really liked the Mikoyan test pilots and had them and their wives over to dinner several times. We were glad that they knew exactly where we were coming from, but this new camaraderie among Russians and Westerners must have been hard for the Ottawa spy world to swallow—their work would have to take on another direction or disappear.

It was at the first German briefing that I told Laurie Dean, our Canadian intelligence contact, my information about Andrei Filatov, the Russian from Radio Moscow who had burst into our classroom while we were at language school. He had already defected to Canada and was working as a broadcaster. Lucky for him he defected when he did, just before the fall of the Soviet Union, when the West was thirsting for any scrap of insider gossip. Now there were plenty of Russians willing to tell all and even discredit previous information. Soviet defectors had become "economic refugees" or just plain old "immigration applicants." Join the queue.

I thought it a bit of a coup to be able to report on the real background of someone who had been taken in by Canada as a "good guy." It was like investigative reporting, or an exposé story. It could never have been done during Iron Curtain days, when it was difficult to check the reliability of stories told by some defectors.

At the paper I had met Valeriy Mikhailov, who had worked with our Radio Moscow interloper. It turned out that Filatov had been quite a Communist whirlwind—the sort who reported anyone who did not tow the party line. Our teacher had been right to be frightened by his sudden appearance: he was one of those "trusted" journalists, the kind who received overseas postings. The journalist I worked with at the *Moscow Tribune* hated Filatov and said he was "the worst kind of Russian."

I meant it as a warning, but Dean ignored me, turning away as though I'd said something extremely distasteful. He definitely did not want to listen. The Russian broadcaster must have told such a good story that his background didn't matter. Or was Dean feigning disinterest? No, there was no indication of a "wink and nod"; something else was going on in that man's grey matter that I didn't understand. After the way he had pumped us up to be information gatherers, I was extremely puzzled and a little hurt.

I was also suspicious. He was an Englishman from a certain era when Brits used to be notoriously leaky. Was HE a mole? Had he known all along about the defector's background and didn't want anyone else to know? There had to be one or two equivalents of Richard Hansen in Canada, or in his case, Kim Philby. In reality, I expect the Moscow radio reporter wove a lot of interesting stories and the military just didn't want to hear any bad news about their "find."

Before Dean turned away, his face had reddened. But I gave him the benefit of the doubt. Okay, I told myself, you have already given haven to this defector in return for his story so perhaps my input that he is not the most reliable of informants is redundant. But the thought that he might be a mole lingered. After all I had been trained by his department to be paranoid.

I was even more convinced when I briefed him on an even bigger story at the next field outing in Germany—one of our own military attachés had been compromised, I told him. This time he listened but again said nothing and went on to talk about other things. Right, so none of this was serious, we were only playing games—as usual.

This particular attaché had been having an affair with a female diplomat at the embassy, unbeknownst to his wife. Some rather strange things had happened to him: his camera had been stolen from his car; his suitcase had been taken from his trunk on his return from a NATO conference in London; and finally his car was stolen. An attaché can't do his job when the KGB and GRU are making it perfectly clear they have something on you. At a dinner party at our house to which Russians and Canadians were invited, an attractive female major arrived as part of the GRU attaché liaison team. She paid particular attention to the philandering Canadian. The attention upset his wife so much that they had an argument in the dining room after the guests had departed to the living room. There was probably already some tension in the home and the GRU could chalk the night up to a victory.

Finally the wife found out and left for Canada. Her husband departed soon afterwards. It probably wasn't considered too serious because the "other woman" was a "friendly," a Canadian. Perhaps Ottawa already knew and didn't need my input. Perhaps they'd had lots of experience of military attachés having affairs resulting from the underlying stress of their unusual lives.

For example, the wife of a military attaché from the Netherlands had a public breakup with her husband. A pretty British woman in her thirties, she had approached me at an embassy function and asked if I could get her a job on the paper. She just needed to do something to get out of the house, she said. Anthony was always pleased to get diplomats working on the paper because it lent an air of credibility and anyway, we were desperate for editors. Like all the editorial staff, she earned a small salary, but I thought that, like me, she would just enjoy the fun of it all. As it turned out that very tiny sum gave her the independence to leave her husband and move in with a young Russian opera singer.

Dean's distant behaviour towards me might have had its roots in Ottawa, where the wife of a previous military attaché to Moscow was suing the Canadian government for back payment of public service pension contributions for the period she had "worked" alongside her husband in the Soviet Union.

She had been a government employee for several years prior to her posting, and of course part of the deal to accompany her husband to Moscow was to give up her job. It also meant giving up her pension contributions, which she now had to make up. She said that as she had been trained by the government to be her husband's partner in Russia and had accompanied him on his many spying trips, entertained his guests (an essential role), taken photographs, and learned a language, she should be entitled to compensation for her lost pension now that she had returned to work for the government.

We were visiting Canada when the court made the final decision. We happened to switch on the television and saw the former attaché and his wife leaving the courtroom. She had won her case, but a spokesperson for the military was saying, "Wives posted abroad no longer perform these kinds of activities." They sure did, but the warning was obvious: without any kind of support from the government that had trained them.

I should have clued in to our new status when the "spouses" were all assigned to spend the day with the wife of the general in charge of the Canadians in Germany in 1993 instead of attending the attaché briefings. But apparently I didn't miss much. Ottawa was a bust when it came to outlining the attachés' future tasks. Because of the breakup of the Soviet Union, the spooks were flailing about a bit. In contrast, American and British attachés were always guided as to what their purpose and goals should be. The French and, to a lesser extent, the Germans were the same. It made life a lot easier than stumbling around hoping to hit on something.

Still, our spy meetings in Germany served to keep our feet on the ground in case we developed swelled heads about all the information we thought we had. It was an unreal world I was living in after all.

22

Man from Gorky

During the Soviet era, Nizhny Novgorod was named Gorky after the writer Maxim Gorky, born there in 1868, and is the place where the late physicist, dissident, and Nobel laureate Andrei Sakharov was exiled. "Exile" in Russian terms conjures up Siberian forests or the steppes of Kazakhstan. But Nizhny Novgorod in the early nineties was a pleasant city with a young, progressive governor, Boris Nemtsov, who actively promoted business with the West. The region's economic success was often held up as an example of what the rest of Russia could achieve. Being a place where cars, trucks, planes (such as MiG fighters), and ships are manufactured, Nizhny Novgorod was definitely worth a visit for foreign spies.

Sakharov's exile there ended with a telephone call from Mikhail Gorbachev in 1986. The telephone on which Sakharov took that call is still in his old ground-floor apartment in a block of flats in a nondescript housing complex. We visited the apartment, now a museum, containing all the artefacts of his life in the city. The apartment was the same as the homes of millions of Russians. We thought, "Hey, this isn't too bad a place to live in exile." The fact that he was forced to live there, under constant surveillance and harassment by the KGB, made the difference.

When Yeltsin later plucked Boris Nemtsov from the region for his own government in Moscow, it was an impossible task to expect him to do for Russia what he had done for Nizhny Novgorod. The tall, handsome, curly-haired liberal politician has remained active in Moscow's political and business circles, but many still scorn him because he was part of the Yeltsin government that caused people to suffer during the market economy changes. He is also Jewish. Even educated Russians will often make a distinction between being a Russian and being a Jew. "You cannot be both," they will say in a tone that dismisses any further discussion.

A Russian black Chaika (this and the Zil were the government limousines of choice before they were abandoned for the Mercedes) met us at the airport, and we experienced a hair-raising ride to our hotel. We hadn't experienced this kind of first class treatment since we travelled about Moscow with visiting dignitaries from Canada. Straight down the middle of the road the driver took us while local police held back traffic at intersections. The driver's tale that he was Nemtsov's chauffeur should have given us a clue that we were being overindulged.

Our first day in the city was very busy. We found ourselves meeting with directors of local plants, with invitations to see cars and airplanes being produced. At one gathering we found ourselves encircled by scientists and factory officials who wanted to discuss their new designs and "talk business with Canada." There was nothing unusual about that—we were used to discussing military hardware, and the latest designs for hydrofoils and ekranoplane fixed-wing aircraft (which skim over the surface of land and water) certainly came into that category. It was all good information, and the visits to the car factory and the ekranoplane plant were immensely interesting.

Then the pleasant designers of the ekranoplane sat us down and with a simple sales pitch implored us to help sell their "dream" to the Canadian government for use on the Great Lakes. Suddenly we felt a little uneasy. When a meeting with city and regional officials touting investment prospects followed this, we suspected something was amiss. Investment wasn't in our line of work. Come to think of it, while there had been security people at the meetings, we hadn't seen a single military uniform. How now to tell them we were only in the business of spying and tittle-tattling, not signing contracts?

On the second day the administration woke up to the truth: it was a case of mistaken identity. We weren't the follow-up delegation they were expecting to a recent visit by representatives of Canada's Department of Foreign Affairs and International Trade. Most of our meetings were cancelled for the second day, but we had already learned more than usual about the area's manufacturing industry. Now we had time to visit Sakharov's former home and get a good look at the city.

Founded in the thirteenth century, Nizhny Novgorod is Russia's third largest city and has always been an economic centre. It lies on the bank of the mighty Volga River where it is split by the equally wide Oka. Gorky and Sakharov are two of its famous former residents, but another is "Russia's Lindbergh," long-distance aviator Valeriy Chkalov. It was because of Chkalov, that we found ourselves in Nizhny Novgorod for a second time.

There was nothing wrong with Soviet Union airplanes and aviators. Both were sturdy, innovative, and gutsy. In 1937, Chkalov, co-pilot George Baidukov, and navigator Alexander Belyakov flew a newly designed Tupolev ANT-25 plane from Moscow across the Siberian subarctic to Kamchatka near the Bering Sea and on across to Canada, before flying down the coast to the United States. They covered 9,372 kilometres in slightly more than 63 hours. The plane was named the *Route of Stalin*. The flight landed at Pearson field, Vancouver, Washington State, and made international headlines. At the time local residents didn't know that the event was history, or that it was the first time a plane had flown the dangerous non-stop polar route.

Years later, one resident recalled, "Here's these three little Russian guys and, boy, were they happy because they had landed … I could tell by the way they were talking they were out of gas."

A year after his historic flight, Chkalov was killed in an air crash. But the region remembered him and erected a huge statue in his memory. For the ninetieth anniversary of his birth, a select number of foreign air attachés were invited to the city for celebrations. Accompanying us from Moscow's military airport at Zhukovsky was the spry ninety-six-year-old Baidukov, Chkalov's co-pilot on that and several other long-distance flights.

It was a cold day in the early spring of 1994, and Baidukov was wearing the heavy grey overcoat and grey astrakhan fur hat of a colonel general of the Red Army. We travelled on a military VIP aircraft with comfortable padded leather seats and tables. With us were the attachés from the UK, India, US, and Germany, high-ranking Russian air force officers, and cosmonaut Georgi Beregovoi. Beregovoi, who piloted the Soviet Union's Soyuz 3 mission in 1968, was also getting on in years, but was as talkative and intelligent as Baidukov. His Brezhnev-style haircut gave him the look of an aging grey fox, and like his colleague, he sported a Hero of the Soviet Union medal on his military jacket.

In Nizhny Novgorod it was minus thirty degrees Celsius, but after lunch we all assembled in the open air downtown for a speech by Governor Nemtsov praising Chkalov. Then a Red Army band played, and we followed it to a high bluff overlooking the Volga River. There, with the sun shining, we watched a spectacular air display of old and new aircraft, including the new Russian aerobatic team of jet fighters. I took photographs of Baidukov for the *Moscow Tribune* as he stood there in the biting wind, his face to the sky.

Our hotel was nicer than the one we had stayed in before, but hidden in one corner of the living room was a tray of what appeared to be kitty litter. A closer inspection revealed that it was bait. For what? Rats I should imagine, given the size of the pellets. The hotel was also having trouble with its heating system. The dining room was freezing. I could hardly eat my hands were so stiff, and there was a cold breeze blowing on my back. But none of the Russian delegation seemed to notice the cold. I had felt earlier in the day that I was coming down with something so at lunch I ate all the oranges I could find in the fruit bowls and I drank copious amounts of vodka. I did the same with the evening meal. Apart from a few sniffles during the night, I managed to stop the cold developing. I have sworn by this remedy ever since.

It was just as well I wasn't getting sick. The next morning we were to take a two- or three-hour journey to Chkalov's birthplace. Although it was still cold outside with snow banks everywhere, we were going to be warm because special Swedish-made buses had been ordered for the journey. Alas, the Russian cold had affected the Swedish buses and they wouldn't start.

We waited. The visit was the highlight of the two days, so the officials were going to get us there by any means possible. In the end it was by two old red Russian buses. These buses started all right, and they didn't have a heating problem because they didn't have any heat in the first place. This made visibility out of the windows difficult because there was frost on both the inside and the outside of the windows. Fortunately, I had dressed in double layers of everything under a heavy navy blue overcoat. I also had a navy blue wool cap pulled down over my ears. During the journey we were all fortified by vodka and cognac and by journey's end we had all become very friendly and jolly.

The bus finally pulled off the highway, and we could make out we were entering a village. The bus carefully manoeuvred the narrow snowy roads surrounding the small wooden *izbas*. We continued bumping along and then turned down a lane to the left and stopped. Dismounting from the bus, we could see a small house and, in the garden, a large barn. Now Chkalov's daughter took charge. We all trooped behind her to the barn. At her knock the wooden door was opened wide and what met our eyes was something extraordinary—the Tupolev ANT-25, the *Route of Stalin*, the very plane that had flown from Moscow to Vancouver, Washington, was sitting in the barn, perfectly preserved.

The western military spies were overcome by the sight; it was just so wonderfully Russian that the famous aircraft from the thirties was just sitting in an old barn in the countryside miles from anywhere. And then the Russian air force officers were also overcome by the reaction from their foreign guests. Russians had spent years and years perfecting how to hide their true emotions in public for a number of reasons, so in the early nineties they still hadn't perfected how to react to outpourings of true and genuine appreciation from their western counterparts. They were learning fast, though, and their surprise soon turned to tears of pride.

Wooden steps had been built up to the cockpit, and we took it in turns to peer inside the three-place cockpit where the Russians had sat for hour after hour as they piloted their plane across the North Pole to America. Although it only had a single engine, the ANT-25 wasn't small. It was some 13 metres long with a wingspan of more than 33 metres and filled the barn in the garden of Chkalov's former home

To have Baidukov on hand to talk about the flight was miraculous. He explained how the airplane had been supplied with a heavy-duty cockpit heater, floatation bags in case of forced landing at sea, and a special coolant system that permitted operations in extremely cold temperatures. In addition the airplane was fitted with special navigation equipment, including a then-unique trans-polar compass, and a short-wave radio with a range of over 8,000 kilometres.

A year before the Washington flight, Baidukov had flown with Chkalov on another historic long-range flight in the ANT-25 over unexplored regions of the Barents Sea, the Arctic Ocean, and the Sea of Okhotsk. It was for that 56-hour flight, which covered about 9,000 kilometres, that Baidukov, Chkalov, and navigator Belyakov were awarded the title of Hero of the Soviet Union.

Chkalov's former home had been turned into a museum with photos and mementoes of the flight. Photographs of Baidukov from the thirties showed that except for a few wrinkles, he had hardly changed. After touring the museum we were taken to a hall for a special celebratory lunch, again attended by Governor Nemtsov. In a toast, Baidukov spoke briefly about his aviator friend and their flights together before thanking the governor for remembering Chkalov and the foreign guests for attending the ceremonies.

The lunch wasn't the end of the special day. Arriving back in the city we were driven to a theatre to attend a performance by the Red Army band as well as singers, young dancers, and performers from Nizhny Novgorod. Baidukov, still in good spirits after his energetic two days, was called up onto the stage and gave yet another speech. This was addressed to the youth of Russia in the hope that they would be inspired by Chkalov's accomplishments.

The theatre was full and everyone clapped and cheered when the foreign attachés were called from their seats onto the stage to stand with Baidukov. Even I was emotional when the Red Army singers burst into well-known Russian and English songs from the forties, specially directed to the men in uniform on stage. The reason people become Russified after living in Russia is directly related to the genuineness of the people they meet.

Meeting Baidukov was one of highlights of my diplomatic experience. He died a few years later and was buried in the famous cemetery of Novodevichy Monastery in Moscow close to the big tomb of Belyakov, his navigator on the record-breaking flights. However, the days of spending lavishly on memorials to Soviet heroes were over. A visit to the grave at the end of the nineties by the German Air Force officer who was with us in Nizhny Novgorod revealed that it didn't even have a headstone: no one knew who was buried there. It was only after much coaxing and urging of senior Russian military officials that something was done to improve matters.

23

Spied Out

Three years, and you're out! Out of the spying game, that is. Although in our case, it was three-and-a-half years because the Russians refused to approve our replacements for months. It was December 1994 before we left. There was usually no important reason for this refusal, and it happened quite often. It could be that the GRU had something against the incoming military attaché (unlikely) or they really liked the incumbent attaché (not a compliment, given his role) or that documents pertaining to the changeover were lost in some bureaucratic paper jam (the most likely scenario).

The extra months were appreciated because it gave us a chance to say a much slower goodbye to Russia and our friends, both local and foreign. We had arrived during the Cold War, had seen the fall of the Soviet Union, travelled through most of the fifteen new countries, and seen the mood in the big cities change from bleak Communism to anything-goes capitalism. I had lived the life of a spy as I had wanted to under the old Moscow rules—covert skulduggery and white lies—and seen it change to almost, but not quite, overt observer, reporter, and goodwill ambassador under the new ones. The period had given us unique experiences and plenty of "firsts," but Canadian military attachés had been coming to that part of the world for years, and we knew our departure would cause scarcely a ripple in the Moscow diplomatic pool.

Most of our work—sleuthing the streets on foot in Russia and travelling to the Baltic states and the "stans"—might seem redundant to action-addicted James Bond aficionados, but we were in sensitive areas at the time a huge totalitarian state was breaking up and no one knew the new rules of spying. We were probably lucky that all our forays had ended happily.

Ever the cynic, I felt that my role—a roller-coaster ride of coups, travelling, interviews, hosting, and living and working on the economy—had entertained me far more than it had contributed to world order. It was Sam who pointed out that governments can react more responsibly at ground zero if they have human spies, however humble, in place who can provide accurate information. He was a believer in the role spies had played in keeping the balance of power during the Cold War years.

Our observations as we travelled throughout the Soviet Union, reporting on the historic breakup and its aftermath, might have impacted Canada's foreign policy. If this was true, I could stop feeling so guilty about those trusting scientists in Siberia during the early days of the Communist collapse: perhaps our understanding of their situation had helped in a small way towards rebuilding their lives.

The experience of living in the Soviet Union changed our attitudes. We understood now why those former military attachés in Ottawa were always looking over their shoulders, couldn't sit in restaurants with their backs to the door (unless they were facing a mirror), and why they went on studying the Russian language and the country's history through retirement. It may start out as fun—"I'm going to be a Smiley, what an opportunity"—but there are enough serious moments, in training and during the real thing, to leave an indelible impression, as well as paranoia. Like previous attachés we had become Russified by our contact with the local people—grumblers and pessimists former Soviets might be, but their stalwartness in the face of adversity can touch even the most cynical expat.

A result of the Cold War's end was that one could return to the former Soviet Union if one wanted to and work in a normal capacity as a business person. My spying days over, I began to take lessons to keep up my Russian with this in mind. The land of the tsars was now the place of opportunity for some.

I returned to Russia in early 1996 to be managing editor of the *Moscow Tribune* for a short while before joining Sam in Kazakhstan. He retired from the military to set up an executive institute for a Canadian university in Almaty, then the capital of Kazakhstan, while I became editor of an English-language business magazine there.

Our training—knowing how to stay calm under strange and trying circumstances—did come in handy. One night about 2 A.M. we were awakened in our fourth-floor apartment in Almaty by the sound of gunfire, running feet, and shouting. We looked out the kitchen window. Parked beneath us was a van and standing beside it were masked men loading machine guns. Paper from boxes of bullets was scattered on the ground. They moved behind trees and began shooting at an apartment building about 20 yards away. The shooting went on for hours. It was being returned, and bullets were flying everywhere.

We kept the lights off and only peered out now and again for fear of attracting gunfire. Grenades were being thrown, and whether they were stun grenades or the real thing, they rocked the area. Then we heard the familiar sound of an armoured personnel carrier approaching. It crashed through the trees and positioned itself outside the building's first-floor apartment.

By now it was almost dawn. We could see the men beneath us wore uniforms of Kazakhstan's interior troops. They were the good guys. Suddenly one of them shouted at whoever was the enemy,

"Throw down your weapons and jump out the window." This was followed by a hail of gunfire. After that there was silence. Around 8 A.M. I went outside to see what had happened. Shocked neighbours were leaving their buildings to go to work, and police and soldiers were milling about. Four bloodied bodies were lying on the ground, waiting to be loaded onto a small wagon pulled by a military jeep.

A Kazakhstani retired general living in our building was also watching. He told me the dead were "terrorists." They had killed border guards at the Chinese border just days previously and had been traced to that apartment. Later I spoke to an old lady who lived across the hallway from the gunmen, and she said she and her grandchildren had spent the night cowering on the floor because of the explosions and gunfire.

While we had been impassive observers of the night's activity, her fright at the fighting was understandable. Perhaps, with global terrorism on the rise, everyone will need James Bond training.

Between our leaving Moscow in 1994 and returning to the former Soviet Union in 1996, I had worked as a public relations writer for Canada's Department of National Defence in Ottawa. To progress and renew my contract, I was told I would need a secret clearance. *Nyet problem,* I said, thinking of my years as a spy with a "top secret" clearance in the former Soviet Union. So I went to the military police office in the DND headquarters, the very same place where I had had my fingerprints so vigorously taken five years before.

"Never heard of you" and "there is no record of your fingerprints or clearance" were their responses after several weeks of me pursuing the subject. Was I so secret that I was in a "for your eyes only" file? Were the clearances issued to wives white lies, not officially "top secret" at all but just a verbal sweetener for unpaid work? Had the enthusiastic, supportive roles of Canadian military wives in the former Soviet Union been quietly shelved following a certain court decision?

Except for the loss of my writing contract, I didn't mind if I wasn't in their files. If there was no record of me ever being a spy for the Canadian government when I was a diplomat, journalist, hostess, and wife in Moscow, then I could write a book—about all the exciting things that never really happened!